PILGRIMAGE AND PROMISE

Michael Marshall was born in Lincoln in 1936, and was educated at Lincoln School, where he was both Head of House and Head of School. He was Tancred Scholar at Christ's College, Cambridge, where he read History and Theology.

He studied at Cuddesdon Theological College, 1958–60, was ordained deacon in 1960, and was curate at St Peter's, Spring Hill, Birmingham 1960–62. Then followed two years as Tutor at Ely Theological College and as a Minor Canon of Ely Cathedral, until in 1964 he became Chaplain in London University. In 1969 Michael Marshall became Vicar of All Saints', Margaret Street, London, where he continued to draw large congregations of young people. During this period he was Founder and Director of the Institute of Christian Studies, and was Founder and co-Editor of *Christian*, a magazine focusing on the needs of the contemporary Christian layman.

In September 1975 Michael Marshall was appointed Bishop of Woolwich.

He is co-author of *A Pattern of Faith* (1966) and author of *Glory Under Your Feet* (1978).

PILGRIMAGE AND PROMISE

Michael Marshall
Bishop of Woolwich

*With a Foreword by the
Archbishop of Canterbury*

Collins
FOUNT PAPERBACKS
in association with Faith Press

First published in 1981 by Fount Paperbacks, London
in association with Faith Press

© Michael Marshall 1981

Made and printed in Great Britain by William
Collins Sons & Co Ltd, Glasgow

'Thither we make our way, still as pilgrims,
not yet at rest; still on the road, not yet home;
still aiming at it, not yet attaining it.'

St Augustine: Sermon 103

ACKNOWLEDGEMENTS

Any writer of a book is deeply conscious that the finished article is not the achievement of a soloist, but rather the convergence of many strands of influence over a long period. In that sense we are all jackdaws taking back to our nests all kinds of bits and pieces which we have picked up over the years.

But, more obviously, a writer is grateful for the more immediate help of others in completing even a small and minor work such as is to be found in the following pages. So a note of gratitude. First to the many people to whom I have presented sections of the second part of the book, either as Bible studies or in retreats. The clergy of the dioceses of Johannesburg, Pretoria, Bloemfontein, Natal and St John's Transkei helped me by their response to some of the content of the concluding chapters during a recent visit to South Africa. The congregation of Holy Trinity Church, Portland, Oregon encouraged me by their warm response during a recent mission in which much of the first part of the book was used. Parishes and clergy in the diocese of Southwark have also played no small part in the kind of continuing formation which is part of the task of writing a book.

But I am most keenly aware of the tremendous contribution which was made in completing the book by the long and late hours which Mary Baddeley dedicated to typing the manuscript, by Peter and Muriel West for their ready and practical help, and also by my sister for the loan of her villa where the main part of the book was completed in peace and quiet and in restful and beautiful surroundings.

My gratitude to the Revd Peter Strange for reading the proofs.

CONTENTS

FOREWORD

'A wandering Aramaean was my father.' These are the very first words of the oldest confession of faith recorded in the Old Testament. From the beginning of the Judaeo-Christian tradition, the idea of human life as a journey to God has been a fertile source of inspiration to the mapmakers of the spiritual life.

Bishop Michael Marshall's book proves that the old tradition is still fruitful. I am delighted to recommend *Pilgrimage And Promise* as the Archbishop of Canterbury's Lent Book for 1981. It is a book that reminds the Church that it must always be a community on the move with a growing edge if it is to be true to itself.

I hope that many Christians will ponder the teaching of this book during the coming Lent, as they make their own journeys to a fuller and deeper participation in the death and resurrection of Our Lord Jesus Christ.

Lambeth Palace   *Robert Cantuar:*
October 1980

INTRODUCTION

Essentially this book is about travelling. It is about life as a journey and about the collisions which occur during that journey. In so far as this book sees life's journey under the lordship of Christ, it is therefore in G. K. Chesterton's sense a book about the cross and resurrection.

> Buddhism is centripetal but Christianity is centrifugal: it breaks out. For the circle is perfect and infinite in its nature; but it is fixed for ever in its size; it can never be larger or smaller. But the cross, though it has at its heart a collision and a contradiction, it can extend its forearms for ever without altering its shape. Because it has a paradox in its centre it can grow without changing. The circle returns upon itself and is bound. The cross opens its arms to the four winds; it is a signpost for free travellers.[1]

There is nothing very original in looking at the Christian life as a journey and a pilgrimage. It is in many ways one of the foundation images of both the Old and the New Testament. Furthermore, it has been a literary device used frequently in Christian literature from writers as diverse as Gregory of Nyssa, Bonaventure, Bunyan and C. S. Lewis. We can regard Christ's own life as a journey from the Father (the incarnation) and back again to the Father (His passion, death, resurrection and ascension). Certainly there is a telling moment in the synoptic gospels when Jesus turns and 'sets his face towards Jerusalem' (Luke 9:51, 53) and all that it will mean in terms of His unique vocation of suffering and death: 'who for the joy that was set before him endured the cross, despising the shame, and is seated at the right hand of the throne of God' (Hebrews 12:2). During Lent and Holy Week the Church turns its face to look in the same direction, and in some sense seeks each year to follow in those footsteps so that we might come to know by continuous repetition the outlines and contours of that journey. For in some ways it must be a part of the journey of every Christian soul if it is to end up by being committed to the life of Christ and ultimately conformed to the likeness of His death and resurrection.

> O let me see thy footmarks,
> And in them plant my own;
> My hope to follow duly
> Is in thy strength alone;
> O guide me, call me, draw me,
> Uphold me to the end;
> And then in heaven receive me,
> My Saviour and my Friend.[2]

But on a journey there are turning points and vital choices when we come to crossroads. Our directions and our compass bearings are important and in some sense we need to know the way before, or at least while, we are walking along the road. These turning points in life, sometimes involving pain, disappointment, loss and grief, as well as joy and love, are never incidental even if at times they appear to be accidental. They are the *collisions* of which Chesterton speaks so eloquently, in which we come up against life. They are not of our choosing. They are seldom predictable. Yet it is these moments which demand change – a change of direction or of speed and even of route: these are moments when we have to let go and move on. They are frequently moments of breakdown, when there can be a real break*through* into a new maturity, and when we can grow and move forward. For whatever progress is, it is not inevitable. As we grow old, we do not necessarily grow – we might regress or just react. Yet if we are to grow we must change: but change in which direction? For not all change is growth and progress, and some change can be part of the syndrome simply of change for change's sake. There is nothing inevitable about growth and maturity – it cannot be simply enough to have a kind of sneaking hope that 'everything will turn out all right in the end'. Life does not all 'come out in the wash': men and women have the capacity for choice – a choice which opens them to a life of infinite joy and love, but equally on the other hand to a life of disaster, destruction and self-annihilation. Furthermore, as the world grows older man's choices have more and more far-reaching implications for the whole human race, until in the end it is not an over-exaggeration to say, with Teilhard de Chardin, that there is ahead of the human race the *ultimate* choice between 'adoration and annihilation'.

But before we get carried away, let us get our feet back on the road. We need to see our journey in perspective and it will be helpful to know something about maps and compass bearings, both before we set out and while we are travelling. 'Pot-luck' and amateur enthusiasm are not sufficient to get you over the mountain passes of the Alps or even over the modest foothills of the Lake District. So with life's journey. Experience and wisdom would teach us the need for direction. The first half of this book is an attempt to take a very brief and inadequately short look at the route. 'This day I have set before you life and death . . . therefore choose life' (Deuteronomy 30:19). On the arms of the signposts are some directions and they involve us in choices at various turning points, roundabouts and crossroads along the way. In a sense we do not choose the road – it is not of our making. But we do have some say in the route that we choose to follow and in the directions that we take. Jesus Christ is Lord of life as well as Lord of the Church. This book is written with a conviction that the formative moments in life's journey, while not necessarily 'sent' by God, are nevertheless opportunities for God and for us:

birth, death, bereavement, illness, and so much of life's
moments of suffering as well as of joy. While we cannot
believe them to be 'sent' by God they are nevertheless
moments which demand our response. They are moments
after which we cannot simply go on 'going on' in the same
old way. Something has to give. Yet at such moments the
road forks: faith or fear; acceptance or anger; response or
reaction; death or life; 'yes' or 'no'; growth or diminution.
So the first half of the book is not unlike the sort of exercise
which even amateur walkers and climbers undertake in
their hotel or hostel after supper on the evening before the
day they are setting out. We need to sit down and look at
the maps and find our references, with their turning points
and their places to stop for lunch and a break. We need to
reconstruct the territory in our mind's eye before we set
out. Such practice is both prudent and also even
pleasurable.

In more complicated travelling it is useful sometimes
to have a guide, whose knowledge and experience of the
route is culled from years of travel and much talking and
sharing with other travellers. 'Spiritual direction', for the
want of a better word, is part of the craft and personal
responsibility of many today – clergy, social workers,
doctors, psychiatrists, teachers and guides of many kinds.
Those people are privileged to be alongside others at just
those moments and turning points when life seems to have
collided with them and hit them hardest. I hope the spirit of
this book will atone for the inadequacy of its content and be
an inspiration to such guides to follow in their own lives a
dedication to this kind of work. Martin Thornton in his
book *English Spirituality* relates how Dean Eric Abbott, in
his days as Warden of Bishop's Hostel, Lincoln, promised
his students that 'if they took moral and ascetical theology
seriously, and continued their own spiritual struggle, then
he could promise that their ministry would be sought and
used'.[3] There is something about the guide in every sense
of the word that is never irrelevant. Such work is a low-key

yet highly skilled profession which is more a way of life than a job, and which takes a man or a woman beyond what could be regarded as the natural exercise of their duty. Yet when people are *in extremis* in every sense of that phrase, and at the end of their tether, they need to turn to someone and there is no one who goes *through* life without that need at some point – namely, a need for a guide who is also a traveller and who has already faced something of the hazards of the journey.

So much for the first part of the book. The second part is practical and limited in its aspirations in so far as it consists of six Bible studies and a concluding chapter. It is a selection of six people who 'bumped into' and 'collided with' Jesus of Nazareth in Palestine nearly two thousand years ago. They met at a formative and turning point in their own journey of life – frequently and literally on the road from one place to another – and in that encounter their life was changed in one direction or another. They are Bible studies and I have often given them on retreats (for the clergy in the diocese of Bloemfontein); in parish Missions (for example, in Portland, Oregon); and in the diocese of Southwark, where I am a bishop, at 6.45 in the morning, to men and women before they set out for work.

There has probably never been such a biblically illiterate generation of churchgoers as our own, and that is in large part because of the multiplicity of Bible translations. That is to say, that whereas our forebears knew whole sections of the Bible off by heart, today even regular attenders at church would find it hard to know and to use the scriptures in this kind of way. We do not sufficiently know the scriptures, 'mark them, read them, learn them and inwardly digest them'. Because if we really knew our Bibles in this way, we should find that the Bible is itself the classic book of life – giving us many map references and pictures of the terrain, and the reports of former travellers with the stories they have frequently told about the route from earth to heaven.

For everyone has a story to tell. Part of the texture of life
is not so much the novels we read and the dramas we see on
television or the stage – they are only copies of the originals.
The originals are the ordinary tales that ordinary pilgrims
tell. Chaucer was right. Life is about a journey and a
pilgrimage, and the tales that are told on the way and in the
way are always the best tales of all. Sadly, today there seems
less and less time for ordinary people to tell their story and
to sing their song, and even less time for others to sit
alongside and just to listen. Bartimaeus would tell his story
of what happened to him on that road just outside Jericho,
until his dying day. As for Zacchaeus, he would be able to
tell you the very moment (to the second) about that day in
the week when he had just had lunch (even what he had
eaten) when Jesus came to stay at his house! But so it is with
all of us. We should perhaps be surprised if we were told
that fairly humdrum happenings (that is 'humdrum' as the
world sees life), yet deeply meaningful moments, were in
fact our deepest religious experiences. We might be even
more surprised if we were told that such moments were
times when *we* had bumped into Jesus, the Word of Life –
Lord of our life and God of our salvation. Yet if the
incarnation of God's love in Christ means anything, it
means at least this and so much more, for Jesus Christ is
'the same yesterday and today and for ever' (Hebrews
13:8). The process is still going on, and still men and
women are bumping into this Jesus on the road of life. That
process will continue for ever, to the close of the age.

But this is also the Archbishop of Canterbury's Lent
Book for 1981. I am honoured that I should have been
invited to write such a book and to offer this contribution
for the consideration of Christians either individually in
their observance of Lent or corporately in Lent study
groups. Furthermore, the diocese of Southwark in which I
serve as a bishop has adopted this book as its Lent Book. It
could be that for individuals it will be a matter of reading it
straight through in the chronological order of the chapters.

But may I make an alternative suggestion? Especially where this book is used as part of a weekly study course it may be useful to combine theory and practice: the map reading and the travel experiences. This would mean that you would read and study the book in six separate and different categories:

Week 1
Part one, chapter 1 and Part two, chapter 1
Week 2
Part one, chapter 2 and Part two, chapter 2
Week 3
Part one, chapter 3 and Part two, chapter 3
Week 4
Part one, chapter 4 and Part two, chapter 4
Week 5
Part one, chapter 5 and Part two, chapter 5
Week 6
Part two, chapter 6 and Epilogue

Such a use of the book would give material for a study group, or equally for personal and devotional study, during the six weeks of Lent. So on with the journey.

June 1980   ✠ Michael Woolwich

PART ONE

DOING THE HOMEWORK

CHAPTER ONE

THE CONFLICT OF CHANGE

> In a higher world it is otherwise; but here below to
> live is to change, and to be perfect is to have changed
> often.[1]   J. H. NEWMAN

In that saying is summarized all that is most promising and
all that is most shattering in human experience. Change is
written into the whole of life, sometimes in tones of
threatening fear and sometimes in tones of hope and
promise. There can be very few people who as youngsters
have changed schools without a sense of apprehension – the
new and the unknown seemed threatening and full of
foreboding. On the other hand, the English climate holds
the promise of a change of seasons from winter to spring
which is awaited with expectation, hope and optimism.
What is certain is that we cannot get through life without
change, and that growth involves change. The pilgrim and
traveller will face many crossroads and forks in the road
before he arrives at his destination.

Change is at the very heart of life itself – it is the story of
our evolution from dust to glory. Organic life, as we know
it, has developed both through evolution and revolution –
continuity and discontinuity – and from time to time in that
story, both history and science have placed firmly on record
crucial moments when life has reached new thresholds.
Frequently there were moments of decisive breakthroughs
into new and more appropriate foms of life – breakthroughs
which had lasting and irreversible effects for the subsequent history of the human race. Science will tell us, and
experience constantly reminds us, that around those
moments of crucial change there was a crisis of

conflicting interests and opposing forces. Nearly all change has been accompanied by the shedding of blood and a decisive element of sacrifice, because there is much that is natural in us which opposes any change in any form. The natural desire is to hold on at all costs to what we have, and to what we have known, for it is familiar, it fits and it is comfortable – like an old pair of worn-out slippers. There is deep down in every cell within us the desire for survival by means of reaction and the hardening of resistance to all change.

Nevertheless, at the same time, and sometimes at the very same geographical location, there is present the conflicting dynamic which both provokes and stimulates a break with the familiar, even a desire for the dangerous – the throw of the gambler or the restlessness of the wanderer. At such moments the pressure builds up and sooner or later the known and the secure give way, albeit only after long resistance and terrifying traumas, to the unknown and the unpredictable. 'The change of life' and all that it implies is written into our whole evolution and into the human story. It is easy to affirm that fact with hindsight, when the victory has been won and when we stand firmly on ground that has been conquered by our forebears, frequently at cost, through sacrifice and bloodshed. With foresight, however, it is not so easy to face the fact of further change on the road to maturity and fuller life. We can applaud the changes of history and the past with the enthusiasm of a revolutionary, but the same voice and the same person will utter cries of opposition and conservative caution when faced with the challenge of contemporary change. The fact of change is an uncomfortable and divisive factor in human experience, not only cutting across the groupings of family, class and background, but dividing us within ourselves, with a pain and conflict which is continuing and seldom absent from human life and yet perhaps not sufficiently appreciated or evaluated as an explanation for much human conduct.

The power of the familiar to hold us firmly in its grip is one of the dynamics within everyone, and only a fool would pretend that he or she has never been strongly motivated by it. There is a warmth and security in the old and the known and the tried ways of life. Part of the power of nostalgia is that it makes no demands upon us to go outside the territory with which we are already familiar. We covet those moments, those places and experiences which have affirmed us in the past, speaking inevitably of 'the good old days'. It is not uncommon for people later in life to return to their roots, as though for them the golden age was in the past, and to speak of their birthplace and early life in ways which scarcely resemble the hard facts of the truth as it really was. More seriously, the past and the familiar can imprison people and fixate them, making it impossible for them to grow because they cannot let go and change: 'Even a prison can become a friend' (Emily Dickinson). The children of Israel, when offered freedom, the unknown and the pilgrimage, soon began to 'murmur' and long again for the security, routine and familiar bondage of Egypt. At least they used to know where they were! It might not have been paradise, but the routine had much to commend it! (viz. Exodus 16:2ff).

At the end of the day we probably have to acknowledge that it is either unnatural or supernatural to go out to meet change willingly and to embrace it. What is certain is that natural man, left to his own devices, prefers the familiar, to stay at home, carpet slippers and all, rather than to go out to face the cold winds of the lonely road, the unknown and the uncharted mountains. To most of us, most of the time, the prospect of change, either in outward surroundings or in inward attitudes, is linked, as it is for the hymn-writer, with 'decay', and there is an inbuilt resistance whenever we are faced with it or challenged by it ('Change and decay in all around I see'[2]).

'A bird in the hand is worth two in the bush' is in a way just common sense; and 'the devil you know is better than the devil you don't know', is the cry of natural man left to himself. Faith and religion at some point demand the opposite. For religious history begins in fact with the 'Abrahamic factor' – the willingness to go out into the unknown. The 'Abrahamic factor' is the basis of all new life – the faith to set out, leaving behind all that is known and familiar, not even knowing where you are going. That quality of faith is *the* essential ingredient (as it was for Columbus) in finding the new life in the new world. But this sort of attitude is either unnatural or it is supernatural: it is never just straightforward and natural – plain common sense. Common sense would tell you to hold on to what you have and to stay where you are. The disturbed people – disturbed by fear or by faith – these will be the explorers, the marginal people who go a bit too far, to the edges of life, only to discover (as Columbus did) that instead of falling off the edge you find a new centre, with new life and new potential.

'Where there is no vision, the people perish' says the book of Proverbs (29:18). You might think that those who reach out for heaven are escapists who are tired of earth, or indifferent to the challenge of the present moment. But nothing could in fact be further from the truth. History does not remember those who stayed behind in Haran (Genesis 12:4), but does remember Abraham, because his faith changed history. We are *his* children and related to his conquest – we are not related to those who remained behind. History does not remember those who cautioned Columbus not to go too far, but it does remember Columbus because his faith changed history. We are more related to him (in that sense his 'children') than to those who remained behind. They were the escapists, resisting the challenge of a whole change of outlook and a completely different way of seeing the world. For faith and vision are interrelated and the one enables the other to open the doors of perception to new ways of seeing things and to new outlooks. And that always is the way in which the future is created – biologically, geographically and religiously: by faith. Faith and change are two sides of the same coin. Without faith we cannot change creatively. If we have no goal – no vision – no reason to believe in the future, we cannot create that future. We stand still, clinging to what we have, looking back at the past with our snapshots and our tape recordings, 'holding it' in nostalgia. Without the promise of heaven and the future, the present becomes little better than hell on earth.

Our culture and our society are not in a mess because of inflation or the wrong kind of political chemistry, which can be tinkered with here or there to improve the cosmetics of a tired image or an old face. The solution is not in a better deal in the present. But rather the problem is that we have lost the point of life itself. We have lost our future. Life has become pointless. That sort of life inhibits creative change and breeds caution and cynicism on the one hand, or just furious and blatant self-destruction for its own sake on the other hand. Yet no one in their right mind would respond to the challenge of change without faith in a better future – a goal – a new world – a utopia or a heaven.

So when Jesus Christ challenged people to leave behind home and family, friends and security, it was with the promise of a fuller life, a goal and a treasure. When God challenged Abraham to set out and leave behind the past, He held out to him a rich future: 'I will multiply your descendants as the stars of heaven and as the sand which is on the seashore' (Genesis 22:17). Every political thinker since the dawn of history, from Plato to Marx, has known that he needed first to paint a picture of heaven and the future if he was to motivate change on earth here and now in the present. Only change through faith can become real renewal, for not all change is in itself a change for the best. We must not suppose that change is the same as progress, though we know that there can be no real progress without change. We often suppose, quite wrongly, that change and progress are the same. They need not be so and in fact they seldom are. An age which has no religion and no faith will have no goals, and therefore it will tend to indulge in change for change's sake. If change does not necessarily always mean decay, equally change does not necessarily always mean progress.

Change which is progress is the breaking through to the fuller life. In evolution we can trace something of this story. As life evolved from its lower forms to its higher forms it passed through many thresholds of change. It may not be easy immediately to define what we mean by 'lower' and 'higher' in this context, unless perhaps we think in terms of fuller freedom and more options. Yet at each threshold and crisis, there is change – a change which at some point is irreversible and in that sense is analogous to 'death'. The death of the old can give birth to the new. The evidence would suggest that there is much overlapping: the evidence that at each stage there is much continuity and much discontinuity. In man's history there is the constant theme of life through death: a death which is at heart irreversible change. So St Paul can say confidently, in the light of his own presuppositions about the proximity of the end of the world: 'We shall not all die [in the sense of passing through the grave] but we shall all be changed' (1 Corinthians 15:51).

It is at such a threshold that Christians believe Jesus Christ stood. In the evolution of our species He stands as man and for man on the threshold of the last and greatest crisis in our whole history. Christians believe that life is not lived in open communion with God, and therefore that it has evolved as far as it possibly can. Without further intervention by God in the whole evolutionary process we were standing at the threshold of death, standing outside of heaven (open communion with God and one another), pressed up against the door, unwilling and unable to open it. In many ways we were in touch with what was the other side of the door by instinct and by experience, and yet we could not come into living communion with it. Evolution had brought us into this moment and now it seemed that it disappointed us of our most profound and primitive hopes. At every point since the dust had settled, there had been the promise of new and fuller life the other side of crisis and change (death): and now at the very threshold of living communion with God (whether through law, philosophy or religion) man still found himself standing alienated and alone – there was no point to it all, after all. In that sense he was out of touch. It was the end. That is death – a living death. Man has only nostalgia to comfort him – a haunting conviction that the Golden Age was somewhere in the past, since there seemed to be no goal or no point to all that had gone before.

It is through this last and most significant threshold that Christ, as man and for man, has broken, with lasting significance for the future of the human race. This is *the* change of life to which all previous and personal changes relate. This is *the* exodus, *the* pilgrimage, *the* change which gives point to all that has gone before while providing both the stimulus and motivation for all changes and renewal which follow upon it. All history leads to this change and flows from it. The crisis and the change of 'the Christ event' is the hinge of all history. It is the tune and melody of which all else is the echo. It is the crossroads to which all other signposts point. It is achieved by life laid down (as in so many previous patterns of change) in order that new life may be taken up. It is the end which is the new beginning; it is the tomb of all our struggles, yet by the work and power of God in Christ it is the womb of all future hope; it is at one and the same time both our death and our birth. It leaves the past behind and reaches out to the future. It involves the shedding of blood and the shedding of tears, for at the last traumatic moment it is resisted in spite of the fact that all previous achievements have led to this moment. 'Now is my soul troubled. And what shall I say? "Father, save me from this hour"? No, for this purpose I have come to this hour' (John 12:27). It is *the* death which is irreversible and yet which reverses everything else. From now onwards everything is reversed: the best is not in the past but, on the contrary, although it still stands on the other side of death, the best is yet to come. Likewise the Golden Age is no longer in the past – remembered with nostalgia – but rather it is in the future, already beckoning us forward through new changes, personal changes and further change, into the richer and fuller life beyond.

CHAPTER TWO

THE RIGHT CHANGE

When Christians, as they frequently do today, speak of renewal – either their personal renewal or the renewal of the churches – they sometimes abuse the word and make it mean what they want it to mean. Yet properly understood renewal is itself a sign of change – a change which relates those who experience it to the lasting pattern of Christ's passion, death and resurrection. When we speak of the renewal of the Church or pray earnestly for that renewal, we are not thinking, or we should not be thinking, of some ecclesiastical enterprise or some new movement (or least of all of some party within the Church or within the structures of the Church).

We are referring to this once-for-all and yet often repeated process of Jesus Christ – His passion, His death and His resurrection. We are seeing that event in Palestine localized and personalized as it was, now universalized as *the* event of all history, and relating both historical and biological and all other change and renewal to this one crucial and central event. Without this hinge of history all other suffering, bloodshed, trauma and change would have no ultimate purpose – nothing less at the end of the day than 'a tale full of sound and fury'.[1] The word 'renewal' is used so casually today, that it stands in need itself of renewal if we are to rescue it from the vocabulary of banality and lift it on to the very centre of the stage of life where it rightly belongs.

People speak of revival and renewal in the same breath, as though they were the same thing. They are just about the very opposite ends of very different, albeit analogous, ideas. Revival presumably implies coming back to life – of which

Lazarus is the patron saint! Jesus Christ did not come back
to life: He died and He was raised. We should not pray for
the revival of the Church. Revival recalls moments which
have been notoriously abrasive in their energies and
enthusiasms, beating it up and trying to make it all happen,
all over again. Whatever 'the kiss of life' may be,
resuscitation is certainly not resurrection. Lazarus took
what Americans would refer to as 'a round trip', and that is
both the agony and the irony of the whole enterprise –
something of which is reflected in the groans and tears of
Jesus standing at the tomb of Lazarus (viz. John 11:38).
For it is precisely man's predicament that the best he seems
able to imagine is that someone should come back to life!
Poor old Lazarus – all this all over again – there is not much
good news in that. Revival implies that there is nothing
'beyond' which is any better than that which we have
known and have already seen – which is the view of the
writer of the book of Ecclesiastes, for whom revival would
be the best possible hope since there was 'nothing new
under the sun' (Ecclesiastes 1:10). No, whatever renewal is,
it is not revival.

Neither is it survival. 'Could not he who opened the eyes
of the blind man have kept this man from dying?' (John
11:37). Such is the power and the irony of St John's gospel
that here again we are being pointed to resurrection and
away from all the other human alternatives of which man's
survival is perhaps the saddest. Ironically enough the very
last thing the Church of Christ is about is keeping people
from dying – resurrection is certainly not preservation. We
must die many times – daily – if we are really to live a
quality of life which is eternal. Jesus did not survive the
grave – He died and He was raised by the power of the
Father. There is much talk of immortality at the present
time, and even pseudo medical evidence is evoked to
support the view that man 'goes on living' beyond the
grave.[2]

Christianity has been agnostic about this (as indeed were

our Jewish forebears), because in one sense Christianity is not very interested in survival. The thought that we just go on living when we have survived the grave has nothing about it which would necessarily imply 'good news'. Many a sensitive agnostic or atheist would find the prospect of immortal life just too terrible to contemplate – just going on going-on for ever and ever, and never, amen! There may indeed be some evidence to support the theory of continuing consciousness after the moment of medical death (though by its very nature it is impossible fully to prove this theory), but that is not what the New Testament means by eternal life, as we shall see when we look more closely at the resurrection of Jesus Christ in the next chapter. Eternal life is a quality of life, lived in communion with God, *now,* and that is the point of all our struggles and conquests of change over billions of years – it is that or there is no point to it at all. A man or a woman is able to experience that quality of life *now* – the full life, the new life, the abundant life which is the only sort of life which is really worthy of the label 'eternal life'. Resurrection and immortality are not the same thing at all, and belief in immortality would do nothing to motivate men and women to change life in this world – it would indeed be little better than 'the opium of the masses'.

The challenge of Christ is the very opposite of this. His challenge is to help us to 'die' now, so that we can begin really to live now – so that mere survival is certainly not the quality of life for which we should pray, and renewal is certainly not survival – it is the very opposite. Survival avoids the challenge of death and change: renewal goes out through death and change to meet and experience the power of God at work in raising the weak into new strength and in drawing the old into the new. If Christians followed a Christ who had survived the grave, they would be disciples of a superman mentality. Nothing could be further either from Christian claims or historical evidence: Christians have on the whole been little men who by God's power have become great men: they have been weak men who by God's power have become strong men. They have 'died' and they have been changed, and by God's power they have been raised to new and fuller life.

No, renewal is neither revival nor survival. Neither does it look backwards to a Golden Age somewhere in the past which can somehow come back again if we try hard enough. The phrase 'the good old days' is just about the most unchristian statement that we can ever make. It is in fact at root totally pagan in its outlook. For the pagan, all the evidence would suggest that the Golden Age was in fact in the past, and that all history since has been a slow decline in continuing decadence. In one sense, if we are not Christians, the pagan view of the 'good old days' is about the most obvious and natural view of the world that we can hold, where youth and vigour belong to a previous age and where change and decay are synonymous.

William Temple, in his *Readings in St John's Gospel*, suggests that the writer of the fourth gospel is implying something as radical as this in his account of the events of the story of the wedding feast at Cana of Galilee.[3] 'Every man serves the good wine first; and when men have drunk freely, then the poor wine; but you have kept the good wine until now' (John 2:10). All our human experience suggests that when you are dealing with humanity you experience the best at the outset and in the early days, but it is not long before enthusiasm runs out and then there follows that which is not so good and the inferior. Friendship, human relationships and human energies have much of that sort of shape and dynamic about them – at the beginning 'the good' and later that which is 'not so good'. But on the contrary, our dealings with God experience that process in complete reverse: 'you have kept the good wine until now'. In Christ the old pattern is reversed and it is this radical reversal to which the miracle in Cana of Galilee points as the first sign in St John's gospel. In Christ, we can say at every point of the journey, 'you have kept the good wine until now'. The best is yet to come – the Golden Age for a Christian is in the future. That is the true motivation behind change which is a change for renewal: 'you have kept the good wine until now'. The Golden Age is *not* in the past – and neither are the good old days necessarily old days. On the contrary, the Christian experience is perhaps best summarized in the phrase 'new every morning' – 'you have kept the good wine until now'.

But equally renewal is not about doing the latest thing: it is nothing whatever to do with vogue and the latest, the trendy or what Christopher Booker delightfully calls 'the cult of the neophiliacs'.[4] Renewal is not ashamed of taking the old and the familiar which have grown jaded and faded. This is often the very raw material of genuine renewal. For, in the gospels, 'every scribe who has been trained for the kingdom of heaven . . . brings out of his treasure what is new and what is old' (Matthew 13:52). Renewal is nothing less than the resurrection at work, making new things of that which had grown old and raising up those very things which had been laid low. In fact a man, a church or a nation are far nearer by approach to renewal when they have been brought to their knees and feel finished, than at those far more dangerous and precarious moments when their only concern is how to keep going and how to keep up appearances under the impression of a natural vitality, vigorous youth and trendy enthusiasm. It is precisely in those places, and indeed in those faces which bear most of the marks of age and weariness, that we find so often the seeds and signs of renewal. Because renewal is not anything that we do in our own strength. Rather, it is something done in us and through us and is most likely to be most effective when our energies are finished and God's new life can begin: when we have finally been broken down and when the new life can best break through. There is something so final about three o'clock on Good Friday afternoon, and yet that moment of death and destruction was also the moment when the new life began to be at work.

That is why it is so precisely 'Good Friday'. Christ was most operative for our ultimate good, not so much when He was journeying around Palestine, but rather when He could not move, nailed to a cross – dead. Then the power of the Father raised Him to new life – resurrection life both beyond the grave and beyond death. That process of death and resurrection is the essential chemistry of genuine change which is renewal, and it is to be found at work in the most surprising places and in the most unexpected faces. It certainly bears little if any relation to places of our enthusiasms or programmes which are sustained merely by our own energies. When Thomas Arnold remarked in the year 1832: 'the Church of England as it now stands no human power can save',[5] he was issuing to those with ears to hear a clear clarion for renewal. It is a blessed moment for any man, nation or church when it is evident (at last, with defences all down, thank God) that his condition is beyond human hope. It is these very moments when the doors are open (if only now from sheer necessity) to the power of God, and when the words of Paul are vindicated yet again for the millionth time: 'when I am weak, then I am strong' (2 Corinthians 12:10). 'My grace is sufficient for you, for my power is made perfect in weakness' (2 Corinthians 12:9). The year 1832, far from being (with hindsight) the year of the final demise of the Church of England, on the contrary, from a historian's point of view, was the very year which marked the beginning of the renewal movements at Oxford among the tractarians, the tremendous expansion of Christian life among evangelicals, and the beginning of the largest missionary expansion the Church had ever known. It is indeed a blessed moment when we know that no human power can save us. That, if any, can most certainly be the moment of renewal.

Change which is renewal, then, revolves on the hinge of the central fact of all human evolution – the death and resurrection of Jesus Christ. This is *the* reversal which has reversed everything else and is the focus of all human hope. Furthermore it is so fundamental to all human history that it is the centre of true hope and alone makes possible a genuinely supernatural motivation for change. It is a crucial map reference for travellers who are up against it and who are tempted to sit down and settle for what they have got and just throw in their hand and 'go back home after all'. That was the point Peter had reached in the twenty-first chapter of St John's gospel, when he says with a cry of weary indifference – 'I am going fishing' (John 21:3). He was on the very threshold of resurrection, but he had not yet gone *through* it. He could so easily – in spite of his earlier confession at Caesarea Philippi, and his previous enthusiastic protestations that he would die with Jesus – he could still have gone back to fishing and have been stuck there for the rest of his life.

'In my Father's house are many mansions' (John 14:2). That is the Authorized Version translation, but it is in fact wildly inaccurate and greatly misleading. The word in Greek for 'mansions' is in fact *monai*, which were wayside caravanserais, shelters at stages along the road where travellers might rest on their journey. It would be better translated resting places, taverns, hospices or just plain public houses, but certainly not by any stretch of the imagination 'mansions'.[6] If we see these places in our life's pilgrimage as resting places, as both points of departure as well as points of arrival, then we have got it right and we are on the road to maturity through the right sort of change. It is this change which will bring renewal and it is this pattern which we must learn most keenly in all our travels and pilgrimages. G. K. Chesterton reminds us: 'there is a moment when the road points to the tavern: but there is another moment when the tavern points back to the road'.[7] Yes, you have been walking all the morning, and it seems now a long lap since those early enthusiasms when our steps sped so effortlessly along the roadway. As lunchtime draws near everything is measured by the distance to the next pub or tavern. Indeed the road seems now only to be measured on every curve and bend along its way by its distance from the tavern, with its promise of rest, a warm fire, beer and a ploughman's lunch. Then we arrive, footsore, almost on our knees, for a blessed time of rest, reflection and recreation. As we eat and sit and talk and rest we are warm, secure and homely. But before too long, restlessness comes over the assembled group of pilgrims, and now our security seems shattered as we tear ourselves away from the glow of the fire and brace ourselves again for the journey. This is the moment when the tavern serves us best by pointing us away from itself and back to the road of our travels.

Such is the life of a pilgrim – and such is the place of rest and unrest, continuity and discontinuity, change and renewal on the road to maturity. Christians are disciples and it is not for nothing that they were first known not as Christians but as 'followers in the way'. The Old Testament blood in a Christian's veins should always remind him that here we have no abiding city, but rather that we are aliens in a foreign land whose commonwealth is in heaven. The old Israelites were essentially a pilgrim people with tent pegs rather than secure foundations, following a cloud by day and a fire by night. So for Christians – the new Israel of God. They are also a travelling people out on the road. If the Romans 'did', and the Greeks 'were', the Jews 'went'. Christian spirituality is not either doing or being: it is essentially going. We have not yet arrived but we are travelling home to God. The map, with its many and useful references, makes for good homework, and signposts are vitally important along the way: but there is no substitute for getting out on the road. 'The journey has its ups and downs, its pleasant resting places, enjoyed for a night and then abandoned, its rumours of dangers ahead, its unexpected meetings, and above all, the sense of a goal, at first far distant and dimly heard of but growing nearer at every turn of the road. This represents far more truly than any combat the perennial strangeness, the adventurousness and the sinuous forward movement of the inner life' (C. S. Lewis, *The Allegory of Love*).[8]

For the Christian disciple, it is to that 'forward movement of the inner life' that all change is related, change which is continuing renewal, 'passing through things temporal' and letting go of them in order to reach out for 'the things that are eternal'.[9] The historic and specific event of Christ's death and resurrection is related to that process: or rather, to get it the right way round for those who have turned round and learned to see things back to front, all change and renewal, if it is to be formative and lasting, is related to that one central event at the heart of our history, teasing us since the dawn of time, yet made obvious and explicit in these last days in the event of Christ and the mystery of faith: Christ has died: Christ is risen: Christ will come again!

CHAPTER THREE

THE COST OF CHANGE

The story of man's evolution is the story of many crises, thresholds and turning points. The pioneers are rightly recorded in history for they break through what appear to be impenetrable barriers. At each stage the pattern is always the same: the first is followed by the few and the few are followed by the many. That in fact is the shape of all redemptive change: the many are saved by the few: the few are saved by the one.

One of the recent barriers which appeared for so long to be impenetrable, was the sound barrier. For a long time it did not seem possible that man would ever be able to fly faster than sound. As you approached the speed of sound, a wall of resistance built up and the science of aviation spoke of this in almost awesome tones as the 'sound barrier'. But as the Second World War was drawing to a close, fighter pilots in deep dives increasingly often drew close to the sound barrier, and the history of aviation takes up the story at this point. It is the story of misfortune, accidents and death, for many of the early pioneers lost their lives as they almost accidentally flew through the sound barrier. In deep dives, as they approached the speed of sound, the whole plane began to shake violently and frequently would be shattered to pieces. One especially alarming fact was that the other side of the speed of sound all controls go into reverse, so that if you move the controls to go up you in fact go down, and vice versa. Not surprisingly, it was this factor which caused the death of so many of the early pioneers.

But today, thirty years or so later, the passenger aboard a commercial supersonic aircraft can lift his glass of champagne unshaken as he is flown at two-and-a-quarter times the speed of sound, eleven miles above the earth's surface, or even sleep quietly as the inheritor of the breakthrough and sacrifice of those early pioneers. The first pioneers, the first passengers and, from now until the end of time, the affluent parasites: that is the way it always goes: that is always the shape of things to come. The one had made way and broken through for the few and the few will open the way for the many: pioneers, passengers and parasites!

Jesus Christ was the first person to break through the death barrier. In our evolution there have been many barriers, and at each point the pioneers have been few and isolated, making way for the many to follow through and take up the conquest, making it the common property of all mankind. But throughout the whole history of these kinds of conquests it was death which was seen as the ultimate barrier and associated always with the grave – the grave seen as the end of everything, the meaningless end of all struggle and life. It was supremely the grave which seemed to cheat the whole history of evolution and all the promise of the past. For if the grave really is the end of man in the sense that it marks the pointless goal of all his struggles, then the cynic is right: 'Let us eat and drink, for tomorrow we die' (1 Corinthians 15:32).

Yet the sting of the grave is death – death in the sense that the Bible means it, i.e. isolation, alienation, being out of touch with God, with neighbour and with self. If we at least had evidence that the grave was not the end, but that the tomb was in fact the womb of new life and fuller life, then the sting would indeed be drawn from the grave. But let us make here clear distinctions. Mere survival the other side of the grave would not in any real sense bring a change of perspective. It may indeed be true, as we said in fact in an earlier chapter, that man in some form may 'go on living' the other side of the grave, but this in itself would not constitute hope, development or progress. The grave would be little more than change for change's sake – 'all

dressed up and nowhere to go!' It is only if we had evidence
that the tomb could be the womb of new life and fuller life –
what the fourth gospel calls abundant life – then indeed
there would be hope. Then, and then only, the 'change' of
the grave would be seen as growth and development, even
giving point to any pain or bloodshed associated with it, as
at our first birth, when the birth of a child – in spite of
travail and pain – gives place to joy and celebration.

It is essentially the quality of man's life – or rather the
lack of it – which is the sting of it all. The Bible believes that
man is in isolation and alienation from his fellow creatures
and from his Creator, and it is this sort of life (secondhand
life, rather than direct communion with God) that the
Bible is bold enough to call 'death'. It is this sort of
alienation and isolation which so many existentialist
writers have so vividly described and which the Bible sees
as a living death. The authors, poets and artists of this
century have been conspicuously most eloquent about the
alienation and isolation of man (strangely enough at a time
when churchmen in the fifties and sixties were still
purveying a liberal optimism about man – a point of view
more in keeping with the late nineteenth-century liberal
writers than with the events and evidence of twentieth-
century culture). It was even the pop stars of the 1950s and
'60s who spoke, often with a strange knack of poetic clarity,
about the meaninglessness of man's life:

> He is just a nowhere man
> Living in a nowhere land
> Making lots of nowhere plans
> For nobody.
> Doesn't have a point of view.
> Knows not where he's going to.
> Isn't he a bit like you and me?[1]

So the sting of the grave is death – alienation. St Paul takes
the argument even further and roots it back by describing

the sting of death as sin. Man living out of communion with the source of his life is sinful. The Bible strongly distinguishes between sin and sins. Sins are merely a symptom of man's basic condition. No amount of moral reform or new moral striving will release him from his basic condition, which is one of deep alienation and isolation – sin. The word 'sin' in the Old Testament is based on an archery analogy, and it is this analogy which is behind the word sin if we are to understand it properly. When we draw the bow and the arrow falls short of the target, it paints the picture of sin as a state of mind which obsessively misses the point of everything and so falls back on itself in decadence. It is that sort of life which the Bible describes as death, for it is a life trapped within its own limitations, full of promises which it is never free to fulfil because it never arrives, never hits the bull's eye. It never gets to the point of it all but ends up by retreating into ever decreasing circles. In spite of the promise of all previous breakthroughs in our evolution up to this point, it would appear that we are, at the end of it all, to be cheated by the grave because, however highly formed man may be, he is still living a living death – out of real communion with the source of real life, God, and so out of communion with others and even himself.

The Bible believes that such is the basic condition of humanity – sinful. Man's problem is his condition, and the symptoms, as in any disease, are only secondary. Equally the Bible is basic in its remedy and is not content merely to tackle the symptoms. Sin is man's condition: sins are the symptom of that condition. A sinful life is pointless, and a pointless life will inevitably be an obsessive life, lurching from one fixation to the next. The sins will be an inevitable sign of the inward condition: they will tend always to be in the realm of possessiveness and idolatry, because if there is no point to living, the danger will be that we will mistake things, and misuse them, trying to make them what they can never in fact be. We will give a significance to things and a value to things and people which they cannot really sustain, because they were not made for that purpose. We shall essentially confuse means for ends, and turn icons into idols. Little wonder that there is the insistence in the Johannine epistles: 'Little children, keep yourselves from idols' (1 John 5:21). For that is so much at the heart of man's wrong turnings. Nevertheless, the solution does not lie simply in tackling the symptoms but rather in changing the whole basic condition and outlook of man. Merely stepping up the rules, or even the sanctions (be it hell-fire preaching) will not really go to the root of the problem. In this sense, Christianity is radical because it seeks to go to the root of man's condition (sin) by a new revelation of God's love and by giving to man the target and purpose of all life: reunion with God in Christ, and through Christ a new sense of order and purpose to what is otherwise a fragmented life. In a fragmented life first one part of the whole and then another part of the whole will play the tyrant in a humpty-dumpty experience of passing enthusiasms. For it is not true that the man who does not believe in God is godless: would that it were! On the contrary, the man who does not believe in the one true and living God creates his own gods, and first this obsession and then that obsession takes the place of unconditional worship and adoration. The godless man will have his tin gods, and homespun, do-it-yourself gods of his own making which break his heart when they ultimately fail him. All these are the symptoms of the disappointed and misguided worshipper: in a word, they are sins.

But the opposite of this condition is what the Bible describes as purity of heart – singleness of mind and purpose. Kierkegaard defines purity of heart as 'willing one thing'.[2] When a man or woman has found that singleness of purpose in the person of the *living* God, all the fragmented pieces are drawn into a single whole around this purity of heart: God becomes the keystone of their life, around which all else is given cohesion and purpose. In the Middle

Ages the Church spoke of this kind of fragmentation, and the tyranny of the part over the whole, as heresy. It saw it not only as misguided ideas and thoughts about God, but as a really basic disease at the root of so much evil in man's experience. There would be much in modern psychology and medicine to support the medieval concept of heresy when it is seen in this way. The opposite to heresy is catholicity – a wholeness and an overriding purpose which brings reconciliation between all the fragmented parts of man's experience and enables him to live his life with direction and purpose. So 'to the pure' in heart – in that sense – 'all things are pure' (Titus 1:15). In such experience sin has been defeated (we are free from 'the slavery of sin'), as we say in the contemporary liturgy. From then onwards we are free to touch and enjoy the world and to use it for what it is – an icon and a very precious and beautiful icon at that. Nevertheless, it is an icon because like all icons it points beyond itself to the purpose of it all. Thus, set free from 'the bondage of sin' we are now free to explore and enjoy because we are no longer in danger of missing the point and confusing the means for the end.

So until and unless sin, in this sense, is tackled, life is but a living death: the 'wages of sin is death' (Romans 6:23). Therefore in spite of all the most wonderful breakthroughs in our history up to date and in our evolution – whether it be biological, scientific or psychological – the Bible is unremitting in its insistence that we are eventually and inevitably to be cheated by sin in the sense described above. We see the evidence of this at its starkest in the sort of life which the Bible describes as 'death', and of which the grave is the outward and visible sign. However highly developed and formed man may be, he is still living a living death – a pointless fragmented life – out of real communion with the source of real life. It is a secondhand existence at best, for he is out of communion with the origin of life and therefore he is disjointed and disconnected, not only with God but with others and even with his true self. In that sense he has lost his roots, and although a rootless plant may still be able to give the outward and visible signs of life for a short time, inevitably it is a plant which must wither for it has not the source of true life within it. Flowers cut from their roots are all right for decoration, but they are severed from the source of their life and inevitably wither. Man does not know who he is, because he does not know where he is going.

Because in fact man, compared with his universal environment, is insignificant and pathetic – minute in a vast universe; weak, compared with the elements of water, wind and fire; irrelevant in his small span of life compared with the millions of light years of the universe. It is only man's capacity and potentiality to have a living relationship with God which gives him stature and significance. It is that relationship which alone can raise man above his environment and his roots, and it is that stature and significance which the Bible calls real life: abundant life – eternal life. 'And this is eternal life, that they know thee the only true God, and Jesus Christ whom thou hast sent' (John 17:3).

Yet it is precisely this quality of life which is beyond man's reach – for man is imprisoned within the death of sin. The Bible, in fact, sees death then as this barrier between God and man, albeit with the handle of the dividing door on man's side, yet man strangely paralysed and unable or unwilling to open the door of division. We believe that God has been knocking at the door of our hearts from His side since the dawning of time. In so many ways God's gentle but persistent reminder of His life, with its abundance and beauty, has always been in evidence through the inclination in man towards the noble, the beautiful, towards truth and love at its best and highest. The irony and agony of man's plight, especially expressed in great art, rests precisely at this point: everything to live with and nothing to live for: a life latent and even heavy with promises which man unaided cannot fulfil. He is finally and always cheated by the grave.

So the good news of the Gospel is God's initiative in opening 'the door of death'. We believe that Christ left everything and came to our world, as man and for man, *to be on our side*: He was flesh of our flesh and bone of our bone and as the pioneer of the human race – from our side – He broke through the wall of partition between God and man – the barrier of death. He returned to the Father, through death, as man and for man, to be the first man through the barrier of death in heaven, at home with God. This divine activity alone was able to restore open communion between man and God, for Christ by His ascension and glorification goes ahead to prepare a place for our humanity to rest in the heart of God. The pioneer of our redemption is through the barrier; the passengers, and even the parasites, are invited now to follow.

This is the goal of all man's struggles and journeyings and it is the resurrection, ascension and glorification of man in Christ which gives point to the whole history of our evolution – for without it our evolution is ultimately pointless. 'Let me not be disappointed of my hope' is the heartfelt cry not only of the psalmist (viz. Psalm 119:116), but of every atom in the universe and every human spirit. Furthermore it is this breakthrough of Christ our pioneer which is the definitive change, both interpreting and directing all previous changes which have gone before; for it is a change of heart and even a change of direction, re-routing us away from cautious and selfish attitudes of self-preservation and mere survival, and opening us to the risk of faith, sacrifice and self-surrender. Only something as radical and far-reaching as this new outlook and perspective makes possible this new pattern of a Godward change in the heart of man. This is renewal because this is resurrection. It is this change and apparent contradiction on which Christ is most insistent in His repeated commands, and it forms the texture of Christ's teaching and challenge: 'For whoever would save his life will lose it; and whoever loses his life for my sake and the gospel's will save it' (Mark

8:35). This change is a kind of reversal, not unlike the
terrifying reversal in controls which accompanied the
moments of passing through the sound barrier, as contradictory and as challenging as the prototype of all true
change and reversal – the man who set out leaving
everything behind to seek he knew not what – Abraham,
the father of faith, change and renewal. The Bible is from
cover to cover a story of this pattern of life through death.
In the Old Testament it is a story both corporately and
individually of a people and of a nation who anticipate the
once-for-all pattern of Christ's contradiction of life and
death. In the New Testament (AD) it is the same theme of
all who follow Christ and find again in this contradictory
pattern – but now retrospectively – the place of change as
renewal and life through death. At all the barriers and
crossroads, for each and every one in their turn, it is this
element of contradiction which is uppermost. We keep
what we are ready to lose: we lose what we try to keep.

The Bible is a record of men and women who have lived
according to this pattern of contradiction. It started with
Abraham, because that is the sort of situation in which it
always starts: letting go and setting out (exodus). It is
basically a question of surrendering what you do have in
order to point towards what you have not already obtained.
In chapter eleven of the epistle to the Hebrews, the writer
summarizes the biblical record of the Old Testament with a
list of heroes who had this quality of faith. It is an
impressive list, starting with the great examples of faith and
the contradiction of the sacrifice of Isaac, and includes the
gamble of faith in the earthy example of Rahab the harlot.
All sorts of men and women have tumbled to this way of life
through death, which in the eyes of the world is always
regarded at best as foolishness and at worst as a scandal of
irresponsibility. Yet this pattern of life at heart is a paradox
and it is a paradox which can only be lived: it cannot be
explained. Thomas Merton writes most movingly of this
contradiction which is at the heart of all true life: 'This

matter of "salvation" is, when seen intuitively, a very simple thing. But when we analyse it, it turns into a complex tangle of paradoxes. We become ourselves by dying to ourselves. We gain only what we give up, and if we give up everything we gain everything. We cannot find ourselves within ourselves, but only in others, yet at the same time before we can go out to others we must first find ourselves. We must forget ourselves in order to become truly conscious of who we are. The best way to love ourselves is to love others, yet we cannot love others unless we love ourselves, since it is written, "Thou shalt love thy neighbour as thyself". But if we love ourselves in the wrong way, we become incapable of loving anybody else. And indeed when we love ourselves wrongly we hate ourselves; if we hate ourselves we cannot help hating others. Yet there is a sense in which we must hate others and leave them in order to find God. Jesus said: "If any man come to me and hate not his father and mother . . . yea and his own life also, he cannot be my disciple" (Luke 14:26). As for this "finding" of God, we cannot even look for Him unless we have already found Him, and we cannot find Him unless He has first found us. We cannot begin to seek Him without a special gift of His grace, yet if we wait for grace to move us, before beginning to seek Him, we will probably never begin.'[3]

Christ is the supreme, single pioneer of this quality of life through death – the sign of contradiction, of paradox and of the cross – and in these last few thousand years of our evolution He has broken through the death barrier and gone ahead to prepare a place for all the passengers, or parasites, who will follow 'in the Way'. There is a wounded man in the heavens: He has prepared now a place for man in the heart of God. That is earth in heaven. The other side of the equation is the Church on earth, where already there is a place for God in the heart of man (albeit broken and wounded): a little bit of heaven on earth now. This is the overlapping evidence in our age of which St Paul speaks, for now that Christ is glorified His Spirit has been given and poured out, at first upon the few but ultimately for the sake of the many: the pioneer has now made the journey possible for the passengers and even for the parasites.

The Church is the hole in the heart of mankind, hollowed out by suffering and brokenness yet already making room for God in the heart of man (Pentecost) as surely as Christ has gone ahead and made room in the heart of God for our wounded humanity (the Ascension). It is in this sense that we can pray: 'Thy will be done on earth as it is in heaven.' The healing of the ages has begun.

CHAPTER FOUR

SUFFERING AND CHANGE

Christ's death and resurrection is the change which has changed the whole perspective for the human race. Suddenly in our end is our beginning: the tomb of all our weary and tired enthusiasms has become the womb of new life. It is this change and this sort of 'death' which is vindicated now as real life. We are invited to go out and seize hold of it, as surely and as really as in any sense we grasp a nettle. Death, in this sense, far from being a place of defeat is, on the contrary, the very place of victory: we glory in it, and make our boast of it all day long. 'In the cross of Christ I glory.'[1] The Cross is the tree of life, and is for those who have eyes to see the way of life (1 Corinthians 1:18). All our journeyings now have a new horizon, beyond our wildest imaginings.

In one sense we know a little of this victory by analogy from our first birth. We left behind the security of our mother's womb, which had been the familiar environment of our formation. At a moment of crisis, which in prospect looked more like the end than a new beginning and more like death than birth, we set out, leaving behind the known for the unknown world beyond. Yet our 'death' was in fact our birth. If we had held on to life in the old environment, we should have lost it, but by that formative 'exodus' in which we seemed to lose everything, we were born and cut loose from our mother. We entered the life of a new world through water and blood.

Christ's resurrection has shown us that the world we know now is not a tomb ending with the grave but is in fact another womb. In that sense we need to be born again otherwise this womb would in fact be our tomb, this

beginning would be our end. Hold on to what we have now
and we will lose all: go out to meet our 'death' now and we
will find life – the sort of life in which neither 'death, nor life
... nor things present, nor things to come' can separate us
'from the love of God in Christ Jesus our Lord' (Romans
8:38f). That is true life and it is what real life is all about.
But birth has always demanded an 'exodus' – a setting out
and a going out to face apparent death – a death which when
faced in this way is life – 'life more abundant'. Little
wonder therefore that the cry of the Church and the Bible is
a summons to mankind to be born again of water and of the
Spirit.

This is baptism, and it is, from our point of view, the
turning point of every man as surely as Christ's death and
resurrection was, from God's point of view, the turning
point for the human race. Baptism is the effective symbol of
this turning point for all the passengers, as surely as
Christ's conquest of death (and incidentally the grave
therefore) was the turning point and sign of His pioneering
work. Except therefore, in this sense, a man 'is born anew
of water and the Spirit 'he cannot see the kingdom of God'
(John 3:1–15). Those were hard words for Nicodemus in
the New Testament and they are no less easy for us or for
any generation. Only if we get our map references right can
we see how death and life, drowning and rising, the tomb
and the womb, are rooted around the same turning point in
all our explorations. Then, and only then, can we see our
baptism as a 'second birth' which in reality is our 'death'–
that sort of death which opens out in fact on to real life,
abundant life and therefore eternal life. Again and again we
have to come back to this point of departure, if we are to
grow in the life of the Spirit.

The sacrament of baptism is, then, the very basis of all
Christian life. No life, however virtuous, comes within the
same order of life as the life which has passed through the
death of baptism – because this life is new life, another
whole order of life. That is why Jesus is compelled to say of

John the Baptist: 'among those born of women none is greater than John; yet he who is least in the kingdom of God is greater than he' (Luke 7:28). The kingdom is a new order and a different league. It is not the old life improved: it is the new life. The good life, however good, had brought man to that point where there was only a thin door and barrier between him and God: however, that could never be a window into God's own environment. At best it was a sort of mirror, reflecting back on the old world, and a distorted mirror at that. It gave ambivalent and even deceptive reflections and analogies of God – in that sense 'through a glass darkly' (1 Corinthians 13:12). Only in baptism do we pass '*through* the looking-glass'. Only then do we see everything the other way round, only then has the door become a window which can be opened and through which the newly baptized can not only see something of God 'face to face', but through it he can share even now in the environment of God's love.

Yet even here the Bible is wonderfully consistent in its claim that no man can see God and live. In order to see God and come into communion with Him, we must pass through death as surely as Christ – in order to bring our humanity into communion with the living God – had to pass *through* death (the Cross). That is why Christians regard baptism itself as the essential barrier of death through which they have already passed. (Paul is quite insistent: 'You have died, and your life is hid with Christ in God' (Colossians 3:3).) The Christian life is not just a sort of glorified virtuous life. It is life lived the other side of 'death' (baptism). It is life lived after you have been pushed under three times, and that for most people is the sign of death and drowning. When you have been under three times you don't come up again except as a dead body! The Christian life is the new life lived 'out of our depth' and the other side of drowning in that sense. It is not just the old life with a new outlook and improved cosmetics. The Christian claims that he has already died and that he has been born again. The new life is lived in communion with God, even now on earth, and in communion with and in service to others. 'We know that we have passed out of death into life, because we love the brethren' (1 John 3:14). We are already citizens of heaven: 'our commonwealth is in heaven' (Philippians 3:20).

And so for the baptized Christian, death is behind him. Paul is insistent that the Christian has in that sense already died. His baptism was his death: a break *with* the old: a break *through* into the new. For we have already died and 'our life is hid with Christ in God'. So we must 'consider ourselves' to be 'dead to sin and alive unto God in Christ' (Romans 6:11). The Christian is a man of the Passover. He has been through the waters of baptism, drowned and raised through the tomb which is the womb of the Church.

The new life (real life, first-hand life, in communion with God) is already our true environment. The real renewal of the Church will only come when this sacrament of baptism is rerouted to the very centre and crossroads of life. It is, in every sense, the turning point of all life, and by proper ministry this great sacrament will be the ultimate sign of renewal and indeed reunion for all the churches. There is no doubt that it must be celebrated in the context of faith (albeit sometimes vicarious faith – pledged by godparents). It is essentially a gift and we must not fall into the danger of making the faith associated with baptism into another work of our striving and virtue. Nevertheless, it is important to see baptism in the context of faith, and to move it from the periphery of the life of the Church to the very heart of the Church where it belongs. It is around the womb of the font that the new life of the Church is born, and in every sense therefore the sacrament of baptism must sooner rather than later in our generation become central to the life of the whole Christian community. It is in a real sense the 'passover' of Christians, and must not be relegated to the margin of Christian life or trivialized and domesticized. It is *the* turning point.

'Do you turn to Christ?' Ambrose would have asked
Augustine on the dawn of Easter Day, 25 April, A.D. 387.
For a lifetime Augustine had been preparing for this
moment – all else had led up to this turning point – faith,
study, suffering, fasting, prayer and yearning. And now as
the sun was rising on Easter morning, Augustine, who had
been facing the wrong way (facing towards the west and the
night) and seeing the world from this point of view, turned
from the darkness of the west to the light of the east and the
dawn, saying – 'I turn to Christ'.[2] He was then stripped and
plunged under the waters of baptism, raised up and then he
entered the cathedral as a new Christian to partake of the
heavenly food of the eucharist. He had, he believed, passed
from darkness to light, for it had finally 'dawned' upon him
what life through death was really all about. He had, he
believed, gone through the waters of baptism as surely as he
had passed through the waters of his mother's womb, and
as surely as the ancient Israelites had passed through the
Red Sea – he had been through it! He had, he believed,
already passed from a life which was in fact a 'death',
through a 'death' which was to be for him life – and from
that point onwards would love and serve the brethren as a
Christian, a priest and finally as a bishop in the Church of
God and in the community of faith. In a word, he had been
baptized.

He had been through it. It is this turning point which in
our map reading helps us most to understand so many
other bends in the road, the roundabouts and crossroads.
We need to learn this map reference off by heart, for it is
supremely the 'turning point' of all life. We shall learn it
best from many different stories and from many different
lips. There is the Red Sea. There is Jordan. And before all
that, Noah's Flood and the ark. Then there was Job, or
Isaiah in Jerusalem under siege. There was Jeremiah in the
pit. The Bible is, from cover to cover, a story of baptism – a
story of men and women who have been through it, with
their story to tell, and their song to sing of exodus, passover

and new life *through death*.

Laurens van der Post says: 'If you have not a story to tel
you have not a life to live.'[3] Real life is always 'on the shore
the other side of those formative experiences and change
of life which seem like death. God's people – 'a people fo
his own possession' – are the sort of people who have in
every sense been through it. Most people most of the tim
try to get round it or just get over it: Christians (Christ'
men and women) have been through it as surely as He ha
been through it. 'What he did for us, must be done in us
(Anselm) not only outwardly in the sign of baptism by
drowning, but inwardly, spiritually, emotionally and in
every other way. In that sense we can indeed be baptized
with the baptism with which He has been baptized, and we
can in that sense drink of the cup which He has drunk (viz
Mark 10:39).

Furthermore, the Bible speaks of this as Christ'
'passion'. The word passion comes from a Latin word
'*passio*' which means 'undergoing'. Christ's passion wa
that whole saving event which took Him from His Father'
side and brought Him from heaven to hell and all the way
back again through life and death. Christ, for our sakes, ha
been *through* it and has undergone His passion – all of tha
to be seen as the lasting and formative change of all life
Christ's people in that sense are a 'passionate' people, fo
they are also men and women who have been through it
and baptism is the sign of that identity. Resurrection
people are people who overcome life by undergoing it
'This is the victory that overcomes the world, our faith' (1
John 5:4). So perhaps, after all, we should not be surprised
if the story of God's people should be the story of a people
chosen 'for His own possession', and a people in whom and
through whom this pattern of life through death is re-
enacted.* It is not accidental or just bad luck that

---

* *Passio* in Latin means undergoing or suffering. In Greek it is
pathos. So in that sense Christians are not only passionate people

Christians are often men and women who have had more than their fair share of suffering, and who seem to have been through so much. It is almost as though God does not choose many successful people or complacent people (viz. 1 Corinthians 1:26ff), but rather people, like Job, in whose lives brokenness is evident. For it is through that very same brokenness that so much healing and full life can flow, both for them and for others. In that sense God has 'touched' them, for Christians are a 'band of men and women whose hearts God has touched'.[4] Yet Job is right when he says, 'Have pity on me, O you my friends, for the hand of God has touched me' (Job 19:21). When God in Christ touches us it is with hands bearing wounds of love: it is through the way of the nails. There is no other way to get in touch again. Job is the type of all God's people, and his suffering is not over and against his vocation but it is precisely the door through which he realizes his deep vocation from God.

> How else but through a broken heart
> May Lord Christ enter in?[5]

So it is that the Ascension of Christ prepared the hole in the heart of God for our humanity. Pentecost breaks a hole in the heart of man for his divinity. Yes, God's people are and always have been, in both Old and New Testaments alike, a 'passionate' people – a people who have been through it. In the second part of this book we shall be meeting characters who met Jesus at a turning point in their lives. They came to the crossroads in every sense, and at that point they either withdrew and went back to the old and the familiar – sin and decadence – or they broke through and discovered a route to resurrection. So it was that Christ's invitation was by implication always the same – 'follow me'. The Christian life can never be lived in a discussion group but also sympathetic. In every sense they are the very opposite of apathetic.

sitting by the roadside. It is lived in the company of a band
of disciples – a group of men and women who have been
through it and find their real life beyond. They are ready to
let go and to go on, following in the way, leaving security
for the sake of maturity and seeing His face set now towards
Jerusalem – the place of man's true and lasting peace where
we shall live in direct communion with God's love. The
appeal of Jesus in the New Testament is always to broken
men and women – men and women who were the last
people in the world whom one would, in many ways, ever
have thought to be the pioneers and heroes of new life. Yet
they were the last who became first, for it was precisely in
these men and women that Christ could hollow out a place
for Himself in and through their own suffering and
passions, so that those who were last indeed became first –
first to leave all, in order to find their real treasure (Mark
10:31). In this sense they were men and women who were
homesick for heaven. Some of the people we shall meet in
the second half of this book will be those who were ready
to go through it and to face that change which was to
bring about the great reversal of their lives. Others
delayed and many are afraid to face it and even become
blatantly indifferent to it. Yet in all their journeyings,
the compass bearing they find in Jesus, as sure as any
northern star, is to be found in His own direction and
in His motivation for true life. Jesus becomes for them a
route to resurrection! He is set towards Jerusalem, the
place of crisis, suffering, violence and even death, and yet
that is the same place in which the new life was to be
revealed and in which they, as well as He, would find the
crossroads to the change of life. Little wonder that the
disciples on the road to Emmaus *turned round* and went
back to Jerusalem.

The New Testament does not attempt to explain
suffering in the world – only a fool would try to do that.
'Christianity,' says von Hugel, 'does not explain suffering,
but it does tell us what to do with it.' It is not accidental that

passio, while in root meaning denotes undergoing, also denotes suffering. For in all created life there is a place for suffering however undeserved, and the same door of pain and fear can become the door of faith and new life. In fact it is not too strong a point to make to say that the Cross is the point of convergence between two seemingly opposite and differing experiences: pain and joy, ends and beginnings, death and resurrection.* In all pagan religions the essential sign is a circle. It is only in Christianity that the basic sign is the cross, with its hint of collision and yet with its arms spread wide like a signpost for travellers, pointing out the options that lie ahead.

So our maturity must involve growing pains, and we shall see that creativity and suffering are not opposite ends of a contradiction but are closely interwoven, not only in our experience of creation and in our own lives, nor either quite distinctively in the lives of the obvious creators like musicians and artists and poets, but also at the very heart of the life of God Himself.

For many people, innocent suffering and apparently undeserved suffering are a real stumbling block to faith in the existence of God as Creator. That is because they insist

* I have always been haunted by a quotation whose source I do not know. I do not even remember quite how the quotation came to me. '*The Cross.* The German uses the word "cross bone", and that same bone is called in Latin *os sacrum,* the sacred bone. It is in the area of this bone that the pains of delivery start. The cross, the sacred love, is the mother; upon her dies the son. That is a law to mankind; the son shall not love his mother as man loves woman. Mother and son: that is for a time the closest of all love relations, for the son lives in the mother. But human life separates them from each other, separates them more widely than any other two human beings can be separated. The Son of Man is joined to the Cross, to the mother, only to die. And he is nailed, truly with outspread, loving arms, to those other arms outspread and apparently loving, to the mother symbol, but as though this were not yet enough, he is crucified with his back turned to his mother. And after that he is born again.'

on putting suffering and the Creator at opposite ends of the universe: an indifferent creator landlord, as opposed to a suffering helpless creature. But the evidence does not support this view. Suffering and creativity belong mysteriously together. That is certainly so in the lives of great poets, artists and musicians. So the evidence of Calvary also refuses to put them at opposite ends of discussion. Here again the Creator and suffering belong together. In so far as the creature is not helpless, but is also a creator, he must partake of the character of God, and it would seem from Calvary that God as Creator is also a sufferer, or as P. T. Forsythe says: 'There was a calvary above which was the mother of it all.'

To be a creator – even a co-creator – is synonymous with suffering. So 'after you have suffered a little while, the God of all grace, who has called you to his eternal glory in Christ, will himself restore, establish, and strengthen you' (1 Peter 5:10), and equally Paul sees this pattern of maturity through suffering as part of the pattern for the renewal and resurrection of the whole of creation – 'the whole creation groaning in travail' (Romans 8:22). Our maturity must therefore, to some extent, involve growing pains, for if we try to get around it or even worse try simply to get over it, we shall be maimed and unable to change and be changed. We must go through it. Real life – God's life – is a quality of life at the end of a long journey, during which we have been through it many times, with baptisms and deaths of many descriptions. Each of us will have our story to tell. Paul recites his in such a way that it suggests that he had told it many times. 'Five times I have received at the hands of the Jews the forty lashes less one. Three times I have been beaten with rods; once I was stoned. Three times I have been shipwrecked; a night and a day I have been adrift at sea; on frequent journeys, in danger from rivers, danger from robbers, danger from my own people, danger from Gentiles, danger in the city, danger in the wilderness, danger at sea, danger from false brethren; in toil and hardship, through many a sleepless night, in hunger and thirst, often without food, in cold and exposure' (2 Corinthians 11:24–7) – but also again a similar refrain. (2 Corinthians 6:4–10). Nevertheless, far from this just being a long tale and catalogue of incidental accidents – just one damned thing after another – it will belong to the fixed points and even the shrines of our own evolution, the most sacred and singular of which were those few square yards around Calvary Hill and the Garden of Gethsemane.

But there is hope for the traveller and there is purpose to the journey. The journey and the quest, are to the realm of reality, fleeing fantasy and all that is of our own homespun making. We are pressing on to the hard reality of true life and although it will involve the pains and the difficulties, the frustrations and the warts, it will in the end somehow transcend all of these by picking them up into a fuller reality and into a deeper context – the new life in the new world. As so often, it is in children's stories where we find the really profound things of life best explained. It was the toys in *The Velveteen Rabbit* who had found this secret of life, and likewise, so often it is the childlike at heart who are best able to apprehend this kind of experience.

> 'What is REAL?' asked the rabbit one day, when they were lying side by side near the nursery fender, before Nana came to tidy the room.
> 'Does it mean having things that buzz inside you and a stick-out handle?'
> 'Real isn't how you are made,' said the skin horse. 'It's a thing that happens to you. When a child loves you for a long, long time, not just to play with, but *really* loves you, then you become REAL.'
> 'Does it hurt?' asked the rabbit.
> 'Sometimes,' said the skin horse, for he was always truthful. 'When you are real you don't mind being hurt.'

'Does it happen all at once, like being wound up?' he asked, 'or bit by bit?'

'It doesn't happen all at once,' said the skin horse. 'You BECOME. It takes a long time. That's why it doesn't happen to people who break easily or have sharp edges, or who have to be carefully kept. Generally by the time you are REAL most of your hair has been loved off, and your eyes drop out and you get loose in the joints and very shabby. But these things don't matter at all, because once you are REAL you can't be ugly, except to people who don't understand.'[6]

CHAPTER FIVE

ALL CHANGE

We have seen how life is a pilgrimage and how important it is to travel through our deepest experiences, undergoing a change which is a change of renewal – life through death. Baptism is the once-for-all sign of that fundamental change by which we are able to be passengers following the pioneer of our calling – Jesus the Christ, the first man through the barrier of death. All our evolution has brought us to this crucial turning point, after passing through many thresholds until we reach this, the last and greatest enemy, (death). This has been finally breached by God Himself, from our side, opening up the gate of eternal, abundant and everlasting life – intimate communion with and knowledge of God Himself. This last victory has occurred comparatively recently in man's story, and from man's point of view – not quite 2000 years ago – is all a bit last-minute, we have to admit! But already the overlapping of the ages has begun and already we are beginning to live the end of life even here and now in the middle.

Of course all this overlapping leads to complications for things are not what they seem to be. There was the old self in the old way and that was comparatively straightforward. But now we have come through it. Now the new self is still in the old way so that in one sense it is true to say that redeemed man on earth is not quite all there! Heaven will be that time when the new self will be in the new way and then, of course, we shall be all there! The new life in the new world. On earth we have to live the new life in the old body, and this leads to all kinds of difficulties and all kinds of frustrations. We *are* butterflies, but we are still lumbered with the limitations of the body of the caterpillar. The fuller life which is beyond death and which has passed over from death to life is still waiting to be embodied in such a way that it really will be an outward and visible sign of the inward reality. But in the meantime things are not what they seem to be.

Which would you rather be: not so bad as you look or not so good as you seem?! You might reply, in a moment of naïve simplicity, that you had no pretensions and that you would simply like to look what you are – neither more nor less. Unfortunately, this side of heaven, while there is still the overlapping of the ages, it is not possible to look what you are and be what you seem. Man's dilemma is precisely enfolded within the stark realization – a lesson we can only learn by bitter experience – namely, that we must *not* go by appearances and that all that glitters is *not* gold. Things are *not* what they seem to be.

Perhaps it is not an over-exaggeration to say that the whole fashion industry began with Adam and Eve! When they were innocent there was no need to dress up – or cover up. But in the garden, after they had lost their innocence, they were afraid and immediately began to dress up in order to cover up: deception had begun. Your body could now take on appearances and affectations: you could cover up: you could make up! You could appear to be what you were not, and say (by implication) what you did not mean. But we must be quite clear that there is no going back. It is a false claim to pretend that nudism is a return to reality (and least of all to innocency). Both the rag trade and the fashion industry on the one hand, and strip clubs and nudism on the other, are dangerous half-truths. It is as though the human race were wedged and caught halfway between stripping down and dressing up – neither being the whole truth!

We cannot go backwards, but redeemed man is halfway between going back to the innocency of the garden and going out and through to the glory and sanctity of the city. In the desert of our own self-consciousness we cannot truly express ourselves. We are lame and maimed and to some extent we are dumb and deaf. We have not got the language, the looks or the adequate gestures truly to express who we are and what we are really experiencing. That is why we are able to share so little, and why mankind is so isolated within the limitations of bodily language. In a sense we are looking for a body, but, like Mary in the garden on the resurrection morning, we are tempted to go back to the garden in the hope of finding it, when what we need is to go on to Jerusalem – to the city – where the Body of Christ (sacramental and mystical) is to be found. What is quite certain is that it is no good holding on to this body in the meantime *(Noli me tangere,* John 20:17).

Recently both a book and a play have retold the story of 'the Elephant Man'.[1] The sad deformity of Joseph Merrick who lived in London at the end of the last century, who seems to have suffered from a genetic defect called neurofibromatosis, has been the subject of a number of articles, books and a recent play and even now a film. At the age of twenty-one, the Elephant Man was 5 ft 2 ins tall, with the circumference of his head measuring 36 ins and his right wrist 12 ins; his body was hideously distorted with bony masses and pendulous flaps, mainly on his head, which enlarged as he grew older. The story unfolds of a man with like passions as other men, but who could never express them in human relationships. In the depths of deep frustration he cries out in the course of the play: 'I believe in heaven.' In a piercing moment we see a man looking for a body as an outward and visible expression of his inward nature, and calling heaven and earth to witness to his inward yearnings, which can never be externalized on earth or enable him to break out of himself into valid and bodily expressions of his inner life.

Here is the parable which speaks of mankind's condition. In that sense we are all 'elephant men'. We see in him our own story. We also are trapped in the limitations of a body which only partly expresses who we are. It imposes expectations of sexuality, and limitations of personality, which our renewed spirituality longs to express truly in outward, visible and tangible forms. Music, poetry, architecture, painting and sculpture are all of them attempts to express and externalize in bodily form our inner life. It is not insignificant that the Elephant Man built, during his brief lifetime a most beautiful model of a church – which he called St Philip's – and which he gave to the woman whom he loved. It still stands to this day in the City of London Hospital, in quite beautiful lines and proportions. We, like the Elephant Man, must look forward to the time and state when we shall have a body which is truly and outwardly an expression of what we are, and so in the meantime we cry in tones of distracted hope: 'I believe in the resurrection of the body.' I believe in that time when things will be what they seem and seem what they are: what the Bible calls a spiritual body, not because it is thinner, ethereal and more ghostly, but because, like Christ's resurrection body, it is more real and more substantial, less limited to time and space – 'not like a ghost' – but able to pass through closed doors (John 20:19). Furthermore Christ is adamant: 'Why are you troubled, and why do questionings rise in your hearts? See my hands and my feet, that it is I myself; handle me, and see; for a spirit has not flesh and bones as you see that I have' (Luke 24:38–9).

In the meantime we have – not unlike Joseph Merrick – a projection of all our expectations in a sacramental body which is a token of things to come, but not built by us – given to us or rather loaned to us by God. We have the sacramental body of the eucharist. 'This is my Body which is given for you' is Christ's way of expressing His love for us even now, while we are trapped in the limitations of our physical body.

But we also have the mystical body of the Church, through which we can find fuller self-expression, and through which Christ can mediate His love for the world. 'He has no feet but our feet, etc.' Both these already borrow from the end and bring the goal of man's strivings into the middle of his experience, helping him to hold on to what he truly is, although the evidence would seem to suppose that he has not arrived – and in one sense of course he has not. Nevertheless we need to hold in tension what man is and what he appears to be: '*Now* are we the sons of God: it does not yet appear what we shall be' (1 John 3:2). All we know is that even now we have passed through death to life, that we are, even now, sons and daughters of the living God. 'When he appears we shall be like him, for we shall see him as he is' in His risen and glorified body (1 John 3:2). In the meantime we live by faith:

> Faith is the affirmation and the act
> which binds eternal truth to present fact.
>
> Coleridge

We must seek to be whole and all together even now – cherishing our experience of being butterflies while waiting patiently within the limitations and frustrations of our caterpillar bodies. In that sense we are hypocrites – claiming to be what clearly the evidence of outward vision does not substantiate. However, we must see it that way round and we must keep it that way round. We are not hypocrites in the sense that we are trying to look what we are not. On the contrary we are hypocrites, and St Paul is not ashamed to embrace the word and turn it to advantage, because we insist and protest that we are what we do not seem to be! We are waiting for the gift of a real body so substantial that it passes 'through things temporal' in order that it may not lose 'the things eternal'.[2] It is a substantial body which is so substantial that it is able to break through the unsubstantial and fantasy quality of everyday life. Redeemed, resurrection humanity will be so solid and real that it would make this world seem like an unreal, unsubstantial world of ghosts. C. S. Lewis describes this turn about in engaging imagery in his description of the road to reality and heaven:

> At first, of course, my attention was caught by my
> fellow-passengers, who were still grouped about in the
> neighbourhood of the omnibus, though beginning,
> some of them, to walk forward into the landscape with
> hesitating steps. I gasped when I saw them. Now that
> they were in the light, they were transparent – fully
> transparent when they stood between me and it, smudgy
> and imperfectly opaque when they stood in the shadow
> of some tree. They were in fact ghosts: man-shaped
> stains on the brightness of that air. One could attend to
> them or ignore them at will as you do with the dirt on a
> window pane. I noticed that the grass did not bend
> under their feet: even the dew drops were not disturbed.
> Then some re-adjustment of the mind or some
> focusing of my eyes took place, and I saw the whole
> phenomenon the other way round. The men were as
> they had always been; as all the men I had known had
> been perhaps. It was the light, the grass, the trees that
> were different; made of some different substance, so
> much solider than things in our country that men were
> ghosts by comparison. Moved by a sudden thought, I
> bent down and tried to pluck a daisy which was growing
> at my feet. The stalk wouldn't break. I tried to twist it,
> but it wouldn't twist. I tugged till the sweat stood out on
> my forehead and I had lost most of the skin off my hands.
> The little flower was hard, not like wood or even like
> iron, but like diamond. There was a leaf – a young tender
> beech-leaf, lying in the grass beside it. I tried to pick the
> leaf up: my heart almost cracked with the effort, and I
> believe I did just raise it. But I had to let it go at once; it
> was heavier than a sack of coal. As I stood, recovering
> my breath with great gasps and looking down at the
> daisy, I noticed that I could see the grass not only
> between my feet but *through* them. I also was a
> phantom.[3]

Yes, Lewis is right and as usual has hit the nail on the head. If you ever meet a saintly person there is something real and substantial about them. They carry weight and are somehow 'all together' – all there. For most of us, most of the time, there is something ephemeral about us – we are beside ourselves, and not quite all there. If we want to make a point which carries weight we fall into the trap of having to swear by something or someone else – as though left to ourselves we are not enough.

But in the meantime the Christian, the follower in the Way, refuses to square things and to settle down in order to keep up appearances. It is as though even promiscuity purged of its selfishness and superficiality and fantasy may be, by inversion, a kind of sign of things to come. The language of heaven will be universal – we shall be able to love everyone because we have loved someone. We shall all in fact be able to speak even 'in our own tongues the wonderful works of God' (Acts 2:11). We shall be able to love in a more catholic and universal way, but with substance and commitment and integrity. It is what the scriptures say: 'Let your yes be yes and your no be no' (James 5:12; also Matthew 5:37). We shall not need to swear by anything because we shall be able to substantiate all our yearnings and all our desires, and 'yes' will mean 'yes' as well as 'no' meaning 'no' – with every fibre of our being. We shall not be 'beside ourselves' with distraction, but we shall be recollected – all the bits and pieces gathered up into one whole expression which says the same throughout every cross-section of the anatomy of our personality. That is what true chastity is all about. It is the appropriate expression of an appropriate relationship. For we shall not be without a body – far from it – but we shall be clothed with our spiritual bodies, and those bodies will be true outward and visible expressions of what we really are and what we mean. We shall not *have* a body but we shall *be* somebody, with a name and features truly expressing both who we are and whose we are. We shall no longer be nobodies because we tried to be anybody's: we shall be somebodies because then we shall be everybody's.

All this will be in the city of true and lasting peace – the new Jerusalem. We shall be in a 'city', though, and not in a 'garden' (simply of God's manufacture and giving), nor, thank God, in a 'desert' of only our own disastrous manufacturing. The new life in the new world will be seen in the city where God and man co-operate in the outward and visible expression of a true and lasting community. For the Body of Christ is a joint enterprise: it is not solely a divine fiat, imposed from above, without our co-operation. The Blessed Virgin Mary was invited by the angel to be the vessel in which and through which the body of Christ was to be formed by the overshadowing of the Holy Spirit (Luke 1:26ff). The city of our yearning is a joint enterprise which will unite both heaven and earth in a single project. That is why architects and planners on this earth are so important and have so much to answer for! The world is looking for a body which will enable it to express true community life without being a totalitarian regime. The new Jerusalem will be a substantial plan of God's devising, yet inviting our co-operation in order to give it substance, as surely as the angel Gabriel invited a woman to give her body and to co-operate with the Holy Spirit in forming Jesus Christ. 'Now I would remind you, brethren, in what terms I preached to you the gospel . . . But someone will ask, "How are the dead raised? With what kind of body do they come?" You foolish man! What you sow does not come to life unless it dies. And what you sow is not the body which is to be, but a bare kernel, perhaps of wheat or of some other grain. But God gives it a body as he has chosen, and to each kind of seed its own body' (1 Corinthians 15).

So the Christian affirms continually his belief in the resurrection of the body. Not this body – but a renewed body where the new man will be in the new way, and when I shall look what I am and be what I look: where the fashion industry will be redundant and strip clubs will be just old hat!

We shall *be* eternal life as well as *having* eternal life, but equipped now with a body to express ourselves. Then we shall look what we are and be what we seem. No one will be taken in, because there will be no need to take anyone in. We shall not need to make up, but rather we shall be taken up, the other side of midnight – nothing less than Cinderella in reverse!

The important thing is that the seventh day will be our Sabbath, whose end will not be an evening but the Lord's day, an eighth day as it were, which is to last for ever, a day consecrated by the resurrection of Christ, foreshadowing the eternal rest not only of the spirit but of the body also. There we shall be still and we shall see; we shall see and we shall love; we shall love and we shall praise. Behold what will be, in the end, without end! For what is our end but to reach that kingdom which has no end)?[4]

Sing praise then, for all who here sought and here found
    Him
Whose journey is ended, whose perils are past;
They believed in the Light; and its glory is round
    them.
Where the clouds of earth's sorrows are lifted at
    last.[5]

PART TWO
OUT ON THE ROAD

CHAPTER ONE

BARTIMAEUS:
VISION, INSIGHT AND OUTLOOK

And they came to Jericho; and as he was leaving Jericho with his disciples and a great multitude, Bartimaeus, a blind beggar, the son of Timaeus, was sitting by the roadside. And when he heard that it was Jesus of Nazareth, he began to cry out and say, 'Jesus, Son of David, have mercy on me!' And many rebuked him, telling him to be silent; but he cried out all the more, 'Son of David, have mercy on me!' And Jesus stopped and said, 'Call him.' And they called the blind man; saying to him, 'Take heart; rise, he is calling you.' And throwing off his mantle he sprang up and came to Jesus. And Jesus said to him, 'What do you want me to do for you?' And the blind man said to him, 'Master, let me receive my sight.' And Jesus said to him, 'Go your way; your faith has made you well.' And immediately he received his sight and followed him on the way. (Mark 10:46–52)

viz. parallel passage in St Luke 18:35–43.

The human problem, according to the Bible's diagnosis, is that we cannot see properly. The Bible insists from cover to cover that man is insensitive – apathetic – and in that sense all his senses are deformed. We are blind, we are deaf, we are lame.

Left to himself man sees everything wrongly, because he does not see the world as God sees it – he sees everything from the wrong point of view. So Bartimaeus is no isolated or unrepresentative figure in the New Testament. On the contrary, he represents us all in a symbolic way for he is

blind and 'there are none so blind as those who will not see'.
Furthermore, his view of life is necessarily second-hand: he
has to learn everything from hearsay ('and hearing the
multitude pass by he asked what it meant'). Begging, on the
edge of life, this blind beggar is a picture of the human race
in our alienation from God.

Life lived out of communion with the living God is
second-hand, relying on hearsay when we ought to be able
to tell for ourselves the wonderful works of God. In fact life
lived out of communion with God is not life at all: it is death
– or so the Bible contends. Our trouble is that we are only
half alive, living on the edge of life ('by the roadside'). The
cry of the New Testament whenever Jesus is coming (His
advent) is essentially *Wachet Auf!* Wake up! Yet
Bartimaeus is crying aloud for Jesus and his cry is the cry of
the beggar in ancient Palestine – 'Have mercy on me!' That
cry comes from the heart, and a cry from the heart never
goes unheard by God. How appropriate that the Church
has adopted the words of Bartimaeus and is not ashamed to
use them at the outset of its liturgy – *Kyrie eleison: Christe
eleison: Kyrie eleison*. We need to get everything the right
way round for such is our blindness and perversity that,
given half the chance, we would not even see the point of
these words. It is not that the beggar Bartimaeus is
suddenly shouting spiritual or liturgical things at Jesus of
Nazareth! On the contrary, he is shouting at Jesus what he
had shouted at everyone else for many years in his life, and
he is shouting at Jesus what every beggar shouted at Jesus
in the ancient world – 'Have mercy on me!' He is simply
asking for alms. The Church has adopted this phrase
because, at its best, the Church can see how the human race
is impoverished and beggarly in the presence of God. Like
all good liturgy and worship, the Church took a human and
ordinary phrase and filled it with the reality and significance which went further in its meaning than might first
seem to be implied. So with insistence, perseverance and
repetition, Bartimaeus, the beggar, brings his needs to

Christ and his need is not ashamed to be basic and obvious
– alms, money and food.

That is the nature of true prayer. It is never ashamed to
be direct, to ask and demand from God in the most direct
way. We must not spiritualize our prayer into pious
generalities. We must bring to God our needs as we see
them. In the course of honest, persistent and insistent
prayer, however, those needs will change: they will deepen
and they will grow. They will grow not because they will
become spiritual and bypass our basic needs, but rather
because the very needs themselves will point us both to our
real needs and to God the giver of all good gifts. We need to
be delivered, both as a Church corporately and as
Christians individually, from anaemic and dishonest, pious
latitudes. We shall do this best if we present each day to
God our Father, who knows our needs before we ask, the
basic even materialistic agenda of the roadside and the
ditch. That is where man finds himself and that is where
God came to find him in the person of Christ (Luke 10:33).

But the problem is the age-old problem of the crowd.
The crowd get in the way – crowds always do of course. We
shall never get things straight if we stick with the crowd. It
says in the New Testament that Jesus had a particular way
of dealing with crowds: he only taught them in parables
(viz. Mark 4:10–12). The point is that the crowd always get
hold of the wrong end of the stick. They hear what they
want to hear and see things as they want to see them. The
parables never give you anything to take away – they
demand a change of outlook first, and like the grit in the
oyster they dislodge our comfortable and cosy way of
thinking, challenging us to look at things in a different way
altogether. So Bartimaeus, your first task is to break
through the crowd and to get to Jesus. That will require
ruthless and persistent singleness of mind, something far
more tenacious than some mere passing enthusiasm of the
present moment.

But there is another sense in which the crowd is always

part of the problem. Jesus simply gets crowded out of our own life by the trivial distractions of what we choose to call everyday life – 'distracted from distraction by distraction'.[1]

All relationships, if they are to grow, need time and space. A marriage begins to disintegrate long before unfaithfulness takes over. Disintegration begins whenever one takes the other for granted: whenever we do not make space in which we can just be together. So it is with our friendship with God. We must not let the business of life just crowd God out. We need time and space for God just as much as for anyone and everyone else we know while we are living in a world of time and space. 'Be still, and know that I am God' (Psalm 46:10). In the Vulgate version it reads *vacate et videte*. Not a bad translation of that could read 'take a holiday and look out!' That is the heart of the spiritual life: doing more by doing less. Stop playing God and trying to run His universe for Him! Start to look around you, stop to listen: be still and hear. A crowded diary is the chief enemy of this kind of true activity; yet it is this very sort of activity which is real life, rather than so much else which crowds into our daily routine and which crowds out the point of it all until life becomes 'just one damned thing after another'.

The point of Sunday is not that Christians should copy the legalistic and enforced inactivity of the Sabbath of the Old Testament. The law is a tutor to bring us to Christ. The old sabbatarian rules were useful in order to bring us to this fuller realization of the place of true rest. Sunday for the Christian is a way by which he identifies himself with God, both as a worker and as a creator, in the deepest possible way. He does this by seeing the point of work and creativity, which is that wonderful moment when we sit back, rest and enjoy what we have done. We look at it with pleasure: reflect on it with gratitude. At that moment we are being most 'godlike' for that is what we are told God did after every step in His creativity, when He brought the world into existence: 'God looked at it and behold it was good.'² That should be the chorus which punctuates all work. In our contemporary world we desperately need to rediscover the 'sabbatical principle' of punctuating our life and our activities with rest and recreation in preparation for heaven. Man was not made for work. That is only a half-truth. Work was made for leisure and, in a society in which there will probably never again be full employment owing to increased technology, it is perhaps the particular responsibility of the Church to educate people and help them to enter into the command of the psalm: *Vacate et videte.* Stop and look: relax and reflect. That must increasingly be the rhythm of true life and growth. Many Christians have found the practice of a rule of life a helpful one. It helps them to set out their priorities and to give rhythm to their life. The word 'rule' comes from the Latin word *regula*, which also gives us our understanding of regularity. It is regularity in our life which brings rhythm, and rhythm enables us to dance and really to enjoy our life. The sabbatical principle must be rooted right at the heart of Christian living, and indeed at the heart of the whole of life, if we are not to be destroyed by a meaningless and pointless unbroken activity. To real life and growth there is always a rhythm – what the book of Ecclesiastes calls 'a season' (3:1–9). There is a season for activity, and there is a season for rest. There is a season for aggressive activity, but there is a season for resting at peace. So, Bartimaeus, do not let them crowd Jesus out of your life: Jesus, do not let me crowd you out of mine.

For prayer and Christian life and faith will always demand single-mindedness and persistence. Sometimes, of course, we have set our hearts on the wrong things and we are asking God for the very opposite of what we really need. Initially, however, that is not important. The important *first* step towards true and lasting salvation is to want something really badly enough. And so the question of Jesus: 'What do you want me to do for you?' There is no chance of movement, growth or lasting change until we

have distilled these basic and full-blooded needs. The
Christian life is not intended to thin the blood in our veins
and change it to water. On the contrary, it takes the wine of
our desires and changes them into the full-blooded desires
of God Himself. But that great process of consecration
begins with the power and determination to want and
desire something or someone with every fibre of our being.
We need to bring to God what really 'makes us tick', even if
initially it is not the right thing or an object which is worthy
of our *ultimate* desires.

> i was talking to a moth
> the other evening
> he was trying to break into
> an electric light bulb
> and fry himself on the wires
>
> 'it is better to be happy
> for a moment
> and be burned up with beauty
> than to live for a long time . . .'
>
> i do not agree with him
> but at the same time i wish
> there was something i wanted
> as badly as he wanted to fry himself.[3]

There is no real Christian prayer or faith which bypasses
our desires and our appetites, our hearts' desires and our
needs. Christian faith and prayer in the presence of the
living Christ permit us to begin by bringing our basic needs
and desires to God, and then slowly He takes them, fills
them out, changes and redirects them. But, be quite clear
that the process of prayer is the directing of our desires and
not the death of them. Jesus says and Jesus means: 'What
do you want me to do for you?' And so it was that C. S.
Lewis could write:

It would seem that our Lord finds our desires, not too strong, but too weak. We are half-hearted creatures, fooling about with drink and sex and ambition when infinite joy is offered us, like an ignorant child who wants to go on making mud pies in a slum because he cannot imagine what is meant by the offer of a holiday at the seaside. We are far too easily pleased.[4]

So, at last, in the presence of Christ, Bartimaeus is able to bring to God the fundamental need which underlies all other needs: 'Lord, that I may receive my sight.' Such was the prayer of the prophet Elijah in the Old Testament for the young man: 'Open the young man's eyes that he may see' (2 Kings 6:17). Such is the need of the whole human race – namely, a new outlook. It is not that we should learn to see a different world – that would indeed be escapism. Rather, we need to learn to see the same world, but very differently. That is insight and that is vision. There are all kinds of different ways of seeing the same object. The human body to the cannibal represents a good dinner; to the funeral director, a possible source of business; and to the sensualist an occasion for titillation! All are different responses to the same object and all represent different outlooks. It is a change of outlook that we need, not a change of agenda.

For the Christian 'with eyes to see and with ears to hear', even 'heaven and earth are full' of God's 'glory': everything has the possibility and capacity to reflect God's glory, rightly used and properly seen *sub specie aeternitatis*. But of course if we are really asking to see things from God's point of view it will be far from cosy. Little wonder that Jesus asked Bartimaeus what he really wanted. You should not *assume* that blind people really do want to see. 'What do you want me to do for you?' is not such a perverse question as may at first appear. We must not assume that sick people want to be healed, that prisoners want to be released or that blind people really want to see. The power of sin is its familiarity – we've been this way so often before, it is cosy and we have come to feel at home even in our 'prisons'.

The challenge of the new life lies precisely in the new and the unpredictable. In St John's gospel, the paralysed man who had been by the pool Bethzatha for thirty-eight years was first asked by Jesus, 'Do you want to be healed?' The trouble was that the man did not answer the question, because he simply repeated to Jesus what he had been saying again and again for years and years. It was always the same old story: 'Sir, I have no man to put me into the pool when the water is troubled, and while I am going another steps down before me' (John 5:7). He had been telling that story for so long that he did not really want to get in the water at all. It was a good story and he was imprisoned in its very familiarity. The power of sickness is that we can lose the will to be healed.

No, you should never assume that anybody necessarily really wants to be healed. We have all met people who are conveniently deaf to certain remarks, while others seem to have the gift of selective amnesia! Facts can stare us in the face and we can choose simply not to see them. Indeed, by choice we prefer blindness, or at least partial sight, to true vision, just as much as we prefer darkness to light. It is not true that grown-ups are afraid of the dark: it is the light which frightens us. 'She might have passed for forty-three in the dusk with the light behind her', as Gilbert and Sullivan said.[5] That, of course, is where most of us in fact prefer the light to be – behind us, with our faces in the shadows which are kindly and uncritical in their obscurity. The words in St John's gospel ring powerfully true: 'This is the judgement, that the light has come into the world, and men loved darkness rather than light' (John 3:19).

The Middle Ages saw it properly: there is something about saints which has got something to do with light – it is the true conversion of the heart, in which we begin to see the world from God's point of view. In the early Church the newly baptized Christian turned to Christ by turning from facing the west to facing the east, where the light was dawning. When you turn round you see things differently. You have a different outlook – you are enlightened: 'In Thy light may we see light.'

Thus it is that in the liturgy of initiation the newly baptized are given a lighted candle with the words: 'I give you this sign to show that you have passed from darkness to light; that henceforth you may shine as a light in the world, to the glory of God the Father.'

So now we can begin to see that the story of Bartimaeus in the New Testament is no 'one-off', isolated incident in life: it is what life is really all about. It brings us to those moments in life which are turning points – literally moments of conversion, when we begin to see what life is truly all about. 'O God, now I see!' These are moments of revelation, when we see for the first time what was there all along, when 'the penny drops' – what Bishop Ian Ramsey used to call 'a cosmic disclosure'. At those moments I catch my breath – the word God is suddenly on my lips – inspiration and adoration fuse into an unforgettable moment of truth, of beauty or of love. It is as though scales have fallen from my eyes – 'now I see'. It is at moments like this that the prayer of the Holy Spirit is readily on my lips: 'Enable with perpetual light, the dullness of my blinded sight.'

So the turning point in the life of the prophet Isaiah was when he saw God's glory in the temple at Jerusalem: 'In the year that King Uzziah died I *saw* . . .' (Isaiah 6:1). That was the moment when Isaiah saw the same old world, but very differently, leading to a completely new outlook which changed the whole of his life, a moment of vision and insight – *metanoia* and repentance. The word *metanoia* means a change in the way we see things. Such is a vital moment on the road of life. It is a 'turning point' for the pilgrim, for it leads him in new directions. It is the moment when we begin literally to see *through* things.

> A man that looks on glass,
> On it may stay his eye;
> Or if he pleaseth, *through* it pass,
> And then the heaven espy.[6]

In that sense Christians are 'God's spies'.[7] They have seen
through things and through people, and they have found
God and His glory in everything. The manifesto of the
eucharist is clear: 'Heaven and earth are full of your glory.'
Many young people today have seen through so much. Yet
they are tempted to be cynical. There will be many that say
'Who will show us any good?' (Psalm 4:6). In the end, there
are only really two alternatives for those who rightly refuse
to live on the surface of life and who demand to see through
life. Either they will become cynics or they will become
contemplatives. But the contemplative is not someone who
sits down and does nothing. On the contrary, he is the
person who can see where things are going and therefore
where he is going. The pilgrim must in that sense be a
contemplative – a person with a sense of direction in his life
and actually out on the road, seeing where he is going rather
than just following the crowd and being 'with it'. For that
kind of direction you will need vision and perspective – you
need your sight, Bartimaeus!

But this is no once-for-all moment: it is necessarily a
recurring experience for those who have left the ditch and
with Bartimaeus are out on the highway. 'In Thy light, may
we see light' – because if we were to see it all at once we
should be blinded. Rather, we must first turn and face in
the direction of the light and from then onwards enter
increasingly into full illumination. But the turning points
are the moments of vision, when we are enabled by God's
grace to come into the presence of Christ and to see God
and His world from His point of view. It is all the difference
between blindness and real vision.

Yet, seeing the world from God's point of view is no
pleasure trip. The new perspective is pretty shattering

one-third of the world going to weight-watchers' classes, while two-thirds are dying of hunger; one-third worried about inflation while two-thirds have not two pennies to rub together. True contemplation – seeing the world from God's point of view – will demand action. The Christian does not leave the world to the materialist while he gets on with his contemplation. The Brandt Report is not just a materialistic concern: it is a challenge to *do* something about a world which refuses to see things as they really are. Christian contemplation can dissolve into escapism and fantasy unless it issues in activity – the right sort of activity. Such activity is called in the New Testament 'prophecy'. The prophet is primarily the visionary who has seen the world from God's point of view, and once he has seen it that way he refuses to sit down and do nothing about it. The vision drives the prophet to re-examine life at every level, and in that re-examination to spell out God's judgement and to bring men to a crisis and a turning point in their lives, when they re-order their priorities as a result of a change of outlook. There is no difference between a prophetic Church and a contemplative Church. On the contrary, the one issues from the other. For when we begin to see life from God's point of view there is only one thing to do and that is to get up and to follow Him. ('And immediately he received his sight and followed him' (Luke 18:43).) God alone knows where that will lead! I wonder where Bartimaeus ended up?

Prayer

Lighten our darkness, we beseech Thee, O Lord, and by Thy great mercy defend us from all perils and dangers of the night; through Jesus Christ our Lord. Amen.

CHAPTER TWO

ZACCHAEUS:
REPENTANCE – HIDE AND SEEK

He entered Jericho and was passing through. And there was a man named Zacchaeus; he was a chief tax collector, and rich. And he sought to see who Jesus was, but could not, on account of the crowd, because he was small of stature. So he ran on ahead and climbed up into a sycamore tree to see him, for he was to pass that way. And when Jesus came to the place, he looked up and said to him, 'Zacchaeus, make haste and come down; for I must stay at your house today.' So he made haste and came down, and received him joyfully. And when they saw it they all murmured, 'He has gone in to be the guest of a man who is a sinner.' And Zacchaeus stood and said to the Lord, 'Behold, Lord, the half of my goods I give to the poor; and if I have defrauded anyone of anything, I restore it fourfold.' And Jesus said to him, 'Today salvation has come to this house, since he also is a son of Abraham. For the Son of man came to seek and to save the lost.'

(Luke 19:1–10)

We have all played games of hide and seek as children, and for children it is a harmless enough sort of game. The trouble begins when we still play games as adults and persist in treating life largely as a game – 'the games people play'.[1] Such complications in life mean that superficial analysis nearly always gets things the wrong way round. We speak blandly of a man or woman looking and searching for God. The hard truth is almost completely the other way round. We are not looking for God: it is rather God who is looking for us. Ever since the time of Adam, man has been hiding from God. The Lord God called to Adam and said to him 'Where are you?' for Adam and his wife had hid themselves from the presence of the Lord God amongst the trees of the Garden. So Adam said: 'I heard the sound of thee in the garden, and I was afraid, because I was naked; and I hid myself' (Genesis 3:10).

So it has been ever since. Man in his fear has hid himself from God and from his fellow creatures and even from himself. God in His love and in His initiative has, however, come to look for man and 'to seek and to save' that which was lost. C. S. Lewis suggests that it is about as foolish to speak of man looking for God as it is to speak of a mouse looking for a cat. It is the cat who is looking for the mouse – and he had better watch out!

And so it is in the story of Zacchaeus. We shall find that it is not so much that Zacchaeus is looking for Jesus, but rather that he is hiding from Him and that Jesus Himself has come to look for Zacchaeus. But Zacchaeus is a little man, and like so many little men he has always had the desire to be a big man. The wonderful point about this story is that, by God's grace, he ends up by being a *great* man. Zacchaeus had heard about Jesus and now he wanted to see what He was like, not to see Him face to face and meet Him, but just to get an idea of what Jesus was like. That is so true of our own lives. We prefer to swap images about people and talk about what we think people are like, rather than actually to have the courage to go behind the image and meet them. We hide behind our images and prefer others to stay behind theirs. We do that with each other, we do it with God. So often our religion, our prayers and our worship do not represent a search for the living God but rather an attempt to hide from God.

God wants to seduce us into the desert, there to speak tenderly to us (Hosea 2:14); the devil tries the whole time to turn God's very allurements into ways of hiding from God. Ashamed we may very well be but, finally,

what can we do, if we really want God, but come out
from our hiding place, and stand, naked and defenceless
before Him? The question we have to ask is, do our
pious practices, our spiritual exercises, strip us down
before God, peeling off our masks and pretences, our
false selves? Or is it rather that they are precisely the
trees among which we hide, like Adam, hoping that God
won't see us? If our religion serves to protect us from
God, then let us at least be honest about that, and even
that little bit of honesty may wrest one of the devil's most
cunning weapons from his grasp.[2]

There is so much which can in fact serve to protect us from
a living communion with God and with others – even our
religion itself becomes a safety device. We constantly
commit idolatry by making God and others in our own
image. It is safer that way! Our prayers and protestations
are to a God of our making – made in our own image.

O Lord, Thou knowest I have mine estates in the City of
London, and likewise that I have lately purchased an
estate in fee-simple in the County of Essex. I beseech
Thee to preserve the two counties of Middlesex and
Essex from fire and earthquake, and as I have a mortgage
in Hertfordshire, I beg of Thee likewise to have an eye of
compassion on that county; for the rest of the counties
Thou mayest deal with them as Thou art pleased . . .[3]

John Ward, the Member of Parliament for Dagenham, who
wrote this prayer many years ago, was sincere but
idolatrous. He had made God the way he wanted God to be
– just like John Ward! God, from His side, longs to show us
His true face – and to remake us in His image.

Yet of course the merciful truth is that God does not
reveal Himself, or all of what He is really like, at one go. If
He did, He would destroy us. Mercifully, God hides
Himself and reveals Himself to us only as we can bear the

truth: 'Teach me as best my soul can bear' (Charles Wesley). Nevertheless, in this process of revelation the initiative is always with God. So Zacchaeus's position was reasonable enough: he had hidden in the tree and almost like a *voyeur* he wanted to see without being seen. If he could stay in his hiding place he could keep this encounter on his terms. We saw how when Bartimaeus regained his vision it led to discipleship. We are now going to see how a living encounter leads to repentance. Vision leads to repentance, so little wonder that Zacchaeus preferred to stay hiding in the tree to see what Jesus looked like, rather than let Jesus see what Zacchaeus was really like. Zacchaeus wanted to hang on, and to keep the initiative in this encounter in his own hands. But then Zacchaeus had hung on all his life and had never been able to let go.

'*Zacchaeus, make haste and come down; for I must stay at your house today.*' Christ regained the initiative. Poor old Zacchaeus practically fell down the tree! When had anyone ever asked if they could come to his house? It was as though Zacchaeus was in nobody's address book. Zacchaeus wasn't in anybody's Visitors' Book – he was in everybody's bad books! But now it seemed possible that his name could end up by being in the Book of Life – and that is the only book really worth struggling to get into!

Because from now onwards everything was reversed. He had a completely new outlook – *metanoia*. Repentance – that is the key word in this whole experience. He was, as it were, surprised by joy, and therefore in the gospel account it records that Zacchaeus 'received Him joyfully'. Here is the new perspective which enables us to see things differently, and in the light of that new perspective all our priorities are rearranged. What was first and most import-ant now comes last and is least important; what we were blind to suddenly becomes shatteringly important and heads the list of our priorities. Of course the crowd did not like this, because crowds are always amazingly conserv-ative. Poor old Zacchaeus was all right really – nobody took him very seriously and the crowd was very happy to keep things that way. But now Jesus was going to change all this, and that of course is a very disturbing factor because the new life of Christ is always disturbing and challenging to our cosy and conservative attitudes of preferring just to let things be.

But the Christian is strong in the distinction he makes between repentance and guilt. Repentance is the very opposite of guilt. Guilt looks inwards and is little more, at best, than wounded pride. Repentance looks outwards in the first place and finds its outlook completely changed (Bartimaeus); it is that change of outlook which enables us to have new insights and to re-order our priorities (Zacchaeus). For the casual pianist a visit to a concert at which a brilliant pianist is performing frequently leads him to the experience of *metanoia*. He returns with the resolve to practise more and to give up other things for the sake of the opportunity of pursuing the craft of a pianist. The experience and change of outlook which comes from a brilliant concert appearance results in a new attitude towards the chore of practice. That is what *metanoia* is all about. It is not ashamed to give up things because it sees the possibility of new opportunities in a life of reordered priorities. So it was that Christ's initiative and invitation made it possible for Zacchaeus to make a new start – 'Love bade me welcome.'[4]

And when they saw it they all murmured, 'He has gone in to be the guest of a man who is a sinner.' Unwittingly the crowd had put their finger on the very heart of the Gospel. It is indeed good news to know that sinners though we are, we can welcome to our home and to our hearts the living God. How else could we ever dare to make our communion, or pray with two or three others gathered together with Christ in our midst, if we did not know that God in Christ is ready to come in and be 'the guest of a man who is a sinner'? That is what the incarnation is all about, and yet in many ways it is too wonderful to comprehend. Mere belief in God does not do very much for the believer. What sort of God do you believe in – a remote, holy, untouchable God, above the bright blue skies? But that is not the whole truth of the Christian belief. We believe that the same God who created us wants to indwell us. 'If a man loves me . . . my Father will love him, and we will come to him and make our home with him' (John 14:23). God was ready to come to be at home with us, sinners though we now are, because one day He wants us to be at home with Him in heaven, saints as we then shall be. But He took the initiative and visited us first. 'We love, because he first loved us' (1 John 4:19). But the crowd do not like this. The crowd never do. They prefer a religion which keeps God in His place – as far away as possible – and man in his place. Sacred is for Sunday; secular is for the working week. But the trouble is that for the Christian there is no longer a division between sacred and secular: everything from the incarnation onwards is sacramental. It took Peter a long time to grasp the full significance of the incarnation. In his vision at Joppa (Acts 10:10ff) we come to the real turning point in the whole religious history of the world. Peter was waiting for lunch to be prepared when he fell into a trance and saw a great sailcloth being let down from heaven full of 'all kinds of animals and reptiles and birds of the air'. Peter was hungry and he heard a voice: 'Rise, Peter; kill and eat.' But Peter was still a good Jew at heart and saw two worlds: the sacred world and the profane world – the latter including certain beasts. In spite of all he had come through he still kept his religious world away from his secular and profane world. Then came the voice: 'It is not for you, Peter, to call unclean what God has touched.'

That is the turning point. God in Christ has touched our humanity and made it possible for us to be cleansed and healed and brought into God's own presence. The man in the street cannot understand this, and in some sense does not want to, because if the incarnation is true then there is nothing in the world which can be called secular, private and man's own property apart from God. That sort of religion makes demands on every aspect of life, not just on Sundays, but 'seven whole days not one in seven'.[5] Most of us, most of the time, do not want our religion to get all mixed up with everyday life. We do not want Jesus to be the guest in the house of an everyday sinner. We prefer to let things stay as they are: a religion which does not come a bit too close, because otherwise it might begin to change things and that could be very uncomfortable. 'You stay in heaven and church buildings, God, where you belong but don't start the business of religion becoming part of everyday life.' Religion has got to be different – a different language (Shakespearian or Latin), a different voice (parsonical): religion has got to be different, so different that it does not make any difference at all to ordinary life. 'They murmured': and it has always been the same sort of murmuring: 'He has gone in to be the guest of a man who is a sinner.'

How often we imprison people by our refusal to expect from them anything other than what they have always been. The self-fulfilling prediction which the school teacher projects upon a bad pupil will frequently determine that pupil's future. But when we are dealing with God there are great expectations and new opportunities. His grace is truly amazing, because it opens up new options which past failures had seemed determined to keep closed.

And so, salvation has come to the house of Zacchaeus. It has come to his house not because he is a strong man, but because through his weakness he has found God's strength. He is remembered in history not because he was a big man, but because this little man had become one of God's great men. The world in its self-righteous prudery will always stand by and murmur and mock. It will ruthlessly seek to find the crack in the armour and the flaw in the story. It is only in God's providence that the very door through which so much evil flowed into our lives can become the same door through which Christ is not ashamed to enter with His healing, His forgiveness and His love. And so it is that through the door of the house of little Zacchaeus enters the Lord of Life. Not because of the virtues or strengths of little Zacchaeus, but rather precisely because the need of this little man was God's great opportunity. 'Behold, I stand at the door and knock' (Revelation 3:20). From the dawn of history Christ seeks, and He knocks on the door of the hearts of men and women to gain entry to the homes of their hearts. When He enters, religion is no longer a matter of keeping up appearances – it is the inevitable outward and visible sign of an inward, compelling reality. 'Batter my heart, three-Person'd God,'[6] says John Donne, and so, thanks be to God in Christ, that is precisely what God has been doing since the dawn of history – knocking on the door of our hearts and asking to come in.

There are two original paintings of Holman Hunt's picture 'The Light of the World'. One of these is in St Paul's Cathedral and one is in Keble College, Oxford. They show the picture of Christ knocking on the door of the heart of man with a light in His hand. It is a well-known fact that in the picture the handle of the door is on the inside, and that therefore Christ can only enter, as 'our courteous Lord',[7] at our invitation and willingness to let Him in. 'O come to my heart Lord Jesus, make room in my heart for Thee.'[8]

William Temple takes this meditation a stage further in one of his writings. He suggests that conventional Christians are prepared to go so far in their surrender to Christ – so far, but no further. It is as though they are prepared to open the door of their heart and cautiously invite the Lord to come into the best room of the house of their inner life. It is as though we invite Him in for cucumber sandwiches, tea, the best tea service in the best room. But then, after a while, our 'courteous Lord' grows restless and asks if He may see over the whole house. We take Him carefully, and not without some embarrassment, to the other rooms – with the beds not made and the

washing-up still standing on the side waiting to be done!
Eventually, when we come almost to the end of the tour, He
sees a room which is locked: it is 'private' and we do not
offer to open it up. So much conventional religion has got
stuck at that stage and has gone sour. For Temple suggests
that there is no way by which we can simply go back
downstairs again to return to the convention of cucumber
sandwiches, polite conversation, the best room and the
tinkle of tea cups. Our Lord graciously walks out of the
house: the temple of the soul is left derelict.

'Behold, Lord,' says Zacchaeus. For now Zacchaeus sees
Jesus not just as another visitor but as his Lord.
Repentance is the resolution which changes everything –
not just religious things in our lives, but everything. If
Jesus is not Lord of all He is not really Lord at all. There is
no such thing as my private life or my secular life. Jesus
Christ is Lord. Many people's faith grows dim, and their
religion becomes a weary round of ritual, because they
refuse to succumb day by day to the conquering love of
Christ as Lord. 'When he is our all, he is our peace'
(Benson). Each and every day Christ's love goes forward
to conquer, and we must likewise move on in our
pilgrimage of surrender. We must not and we cannot stand
still. 'Today is salvation come to this house.' Today is
always a new opportunity to surrender to Christ's love –
'Today if you will hear his voice, harden not your hearts'
(Venite).

Zacchaeus's name is remembered in history, not because
his name was in the history books but because his name was
in the Book of Life. Like so many little men he had longed
to make it and become a big man. He had longed to be
remembered by men. In fact no one would have remembered Zacchaeus after the life that he had originally
lived; but the way to his maturity was by quite another
road. He was remembered by God and recalled by Him. It
was in his response and repentance to that call that his
greatness was to be found, and that is a way open to all men

for it is the way which leads to eternal life and we know from the concluding words of this story the good news: 'The Son of man came to seek and to save that which was lost.'

Prayer

Almighty God, give us grace that we may cast away the works of darkness, and put upon us the armour of light, now in the time of this mortal life, in which Thy Son Jesus Christ came to visit us in great humility; that in the last day, when He shall come again in His glorious Majesty to judge both the quick and the dead, we may rise to the life immortal, through Him who liveth and reigneth with Thee and the Holy Ghost, now and ever. Amen.

CHAPTER THREE

THE RICH YOUNG RULER:
LETTING GO AND GIVING UP

*And as he was setting out on his journey, a man ran up and
knelt before him, and asked him, 'Good Teacher, what must I
do to inherit eternal life?' And Jesus said to him, 'Why do
you call me good? No one is good but God alone. You know
the commandments: "Do not kill, Do not commit adultery,
Do not steal, Do not bear false witness, Do not defraud,
Honour your father and mother".' And he said to him,
'Teacher, all these I have observed from my youth.' And
Jesus looking upon him loved him, and said to him, 'You lack
one thing; go, sell what you have, and give to the poor, and
you will have treasure in heaven; and come, follow me.' At
that saying his countenance fell, and he went away
sorrowful; for he had great possessions.* (Mark 10:17-22)

The best is yet to come. The Christian pilgrim cannot stand
still for very long because he believes that, although the
world through which he is travelling is heavy with
promises, they are promises which cannot be fulfilled *in* the
world. All our experiences at the deepest level point
beyond themselves and are incapable of fulfilling their own
promises, unless like a traveller we go ever forward to the
land of promise. So life has become for us what C. S. Lewis
describes so aptly as: 'The echo of a tune we have not yet
heard, news from a country we have not yet visited, the
scent of a flower we have not yet picked.'[1] So if we are not to
get stuck we must travel to the country we have not yet
visited, we must go out and find the flower that we have not
yet plucked, and we must go on to find the music and its

source, ruthlessly refusing to stand still and settle down. The only difference between a rut and a grave is that one is a little deeper than the other. For if we get stuck, however far we are along the road, we shall die. The achievement of today's journey rightly brings me to a point of rest, and I am banging in the tent pegs to settle down for the night. But the dawn and the light promise new territory for conquering, and yesterday's achievements will be tomorrow's defeats unless we pull up the tent pegs and journey on.

'That which is good, sanctifying and spiritual for my brother below or beside me on the mountain side, can be material, misleading or bad for me. What I rightly allowed myself yesterday, I must perhaps deny myself today.'[2] That is the restless impatience and detachment of a true pilgrim, and equally the single-mindedness of the treasure hunter. So the words of Job are the antiphon of the traveller: 'The Lord gave, the Lord has taken away, blesssed be the name of the Lord.' The conversion points and turning points in our lives are moments which are given to us. We must not hang on to them but we must let go at the right moment, in order that we may keep travelling. So often, however, we mistake the means for the end and we try to settle down with truth as we have already perceived it. For Bartimaeus it was important to get out on the road and to follow Jesus. All the most wonderful experiences in our lives go sour and become faded and jaded, unless we permit them to point us to the ultimate treasure, where neither moth nor rust consumes and where thieves do not break in and steal (viz Matthew 6:19).

And so there is a turning point in our lives which is best described by the turning point reached in the life of the rich young ruler. He was earnest and he was keen, this rich young man, as he came 'running' to Jesus to ask Him what he had to do to 'get' eternal life. This young man had always managed to get everything else in life – at a price – and yet all that he had acquired had failed to fill the hole in his heart and a deep yearning for more. Could it be that 'eternal life' was the piece of the jigsaw for which he had always been looking? For he had already travelled a long way on his religious pilgrimage. He was already a keen, religious young man. He knew the rules and he had kept them as best he could since his youth. And now he comes to a turning point on the road in his pilgrimage and he stands with Jesus at the crossroads.

The epitaph on the tomb of this rich young man might well have read: 'Possessed by his possessions: he longed to belong, but he ended up belonging to his belongings!' For let us be quite certain that the nineteenth-century liberals were wrong: man was not born to be free – but rather to be possessed. We shall fill the void in our lives with something or somebody, and yet everything we fill it with will turn us into its slave and become our master. It is only the true and living God who, when He possesses us, truly sets us free because only His bondage is perfect freedom. So in a strange way, which is full of irony, man is certainly not born to be free but rather he is born to be possessed. It is a question of finding the God to worship who will truly set us free, for man is a compulsive worshipper and longs to give himself in adoration and worship. The rich young man in that sense was a compulsive worshipper: he literally adored things.

But all things in this world are sacraments of God: signs of His presence. For, in the end, it is God whom we want. If we travel properly and get things in the right order, we can end up with God and everything else as well. If we get it wrong, however, we shall lose everything. This is an important crossroad: we need to experience a real conversion at this turning point in the road, or else vision and repentance could still leave us hung up and hold us up at this point of the journey for a very long time. Augustine was right: 'We were made by God and for God and our hearts are restless until they rest in God.'[3] And so at the heart of man there is a strange struggle for independence and at the same time there is also a desire for surrender

Like the rich young ruler, we should love to acquire virtues and keep our independence. We should like a religion which gave us goodness but without bringing us to the point where we needed to surrender to the author of goodness – God. In many ways our civilization at the moment longs for goodness, but wants that goodness without God. The rich young ruler thinks that he can begin a discussion about goodness without in some sense being brought into the presence of God – 'good master'. In that way we suppose that we shall still be in charge – in control – and like a jackdaw we shall simply amass a wealth of things, taking them to our nest, in isolation and security. Then it would be religion on our terms. Eternal life becomes another thing which the collector could collect. There is the instinct of a collector in some way in all of us – yet herein lies our poverty. Like the children of Israel in the Old Testament, we hoard the daily bread until it 'stinks' because we cannot believe that God will give us our daily bread and all that we need as we need it. There is a sense in which we become materialistic, therefore, even about spiritual gifts, and we want to possess them rather than letting eternal life possess us. For the food is food for the journey (*viaticum*): it is not to be hoarded.

Yet in many ways this young man was a good man. But then goodness is not enough, for in the end the enemy of the best is not the worst but the good. It was good men who crucified Jesus, not by going too far but by not going far enough. So it will not be our weaknesses which will keep us out of heaven so much as our strengths. It will be our strengths and our 'riches' which, if we are not careful, will keep us most from God. For it will be these that will tempt us to hold back from just that poverty of spirit through which we can alone be made truly rich. For eternal life is not something that we have but something which we are given. 'My song is love unknown my Saviour's love for me.'[4] And therefore it is not surprising that 'Jesus looking upon him loved him'. There is the heart of the matter – not

my love of God but His love for me, leading me on and
weaning me to maturity through that quality of life which
finds its only security in God's abundance and in God's
generosity. In the presence of that quality of love we are
really all poor. So the initiative is always with God. 'You
lack one thing,' He says to the rich young ruler. Can you
imagine the irony and power of that statement? Here was a
young man so rich with possessions that you would never
quite have known what to buy him for Christmas or for his
birthday, and so little wonder that the word of Jesus
unhinges him as Jesus has the audacity to say to this man
that there is one thing that he lacks. Be quite sure then that
this is the understatement of eternity – this young man
lacked just about everything, but mercifully in dealing with
God it is always one step at a time. He had come to the
crossroads and if he had been prepared to take the right
turning now he would indeed have been rich – but rich in
God's grace rather than rich in his own possessions. The
first step in the right direction for the rich young man is to
let go of everything, so that his hands can be truly open and
empty, ready to receive everything back as a gift from God.
In that sense he would have been truly rich in God's
gracious giving.

Here unfortunately the young man got stuck – holding
on, hung up on the gifts which he regarded as his
possessions. It is so hard for the rich to receive heavenly
treasure. It is so hard for the rich to receive the gifts of God
whether they are rich in money, rich in talent, rich in
beauty. They will always in some sense be the last into the
kingdom of heaven, if they can get in at all. For in the
kingdom everything is in reverse: the anthem of the Blessed
Virgin Mary sums it all up when she says: 'He has put down
the mighty from their thrones, and exalted those of low
degree; he has filled the hungry with good things, and the
rich he has sent empty away' (Luke 1:52ff). But we must
beware at this point. We must pray for the rich, we must
pray for the beautiful and the clever, for they are last in the

line and find it hardest to receive anything and most of all the gift of eternal life. So we can begin to see that this rich young man is not rich at all, he is a poor young man, for he is stuck and hung up with his possessions.

> In order to arrive there,
> To arrive where you are, to get from where you are not,
> You must go by a way wherein there is no ecstasy.
> In order to arrive at what you do not know
> You must go by a way which is the way of ignorance.
> In order to possess what you do not possess
> You must go by the way of dispossession.
>
> T. S. Eliot, 'East Coker' III[5]

Little wonder therefore that the writer of the gospel account is at pains to say that he went away sorrowful – fixated – like a record which has stuck in the same groove, or rather like the stylus that has found the crack and the flaw and so has no way forward until the divine hand comes again to move it on.

For there are many points in our pilgrimage and travelling towards God in which He says to each one of us 'there is still one thing that you lack'. There are all kinds of icons in our lives which have become idols; all kinds of means of grace which have become ends; all kinds of turnings which have become dead ends.

> The dearest idol I have known,
> Whate'er that idol be,
> O help me tear it from Thy throne
> And worship only Thee.[6]

All this, not because the things in themselves are wicked, and not necessarily because at the end of the day we shall not still be given back by God all those things that we were asked to give up. It is rather because, in the end, nothing less than eternal life will satisfy us and because if we cling to the things we already have we shall end up by losing those things that God wishes still to give us. So we need to be able to let go, and we need to be able to take the knife to cut the cord which binds us to our hearts' desires. Such was the contradiction in Abraham's offering of Isaac. Abraham and Sarah had set their hearts on the birth of a child, but since they were 'past it' it seemed that such a gift could never be given. So absurd, indeed, seemed the promise of the angel, and the prospect of a child at their time of life, that Sarah laughed in the very face of the angel because she thought it was some sort of a joke. And indeed it was, for it was not long before Isaac was born – the only son of very aged parents – and that might have ended up by being a sick joke. For he was an only son, a much loved son (*agapētos*). They called him Isaac, which means a joke, but it was far from a joke for he was their hearts' desire, and unless Abraham could have got to the point of slaying that child he would have devoured him in the name of love. Once he got to that point, God, far from wishing the child to be killed, wanted him as part of His divine purposes. Nevertheless, Abraham simply had to reach that point where he could let go before God's purposes could in any way be forwarded through his heart's desire – Isaac.

So it is with all our gifts – all our 'isaacs' – all our hearts' desires. Sooner or later we must be set free from them and they from us, not because they are bad in themselves, but precisely because they are good and need to become the best or they will deteriorate into the worst. All our gifts and talents need redeeming and we can do it best by thanking God for them and being able to let go of them in order to receive them back for what they truly are – God's gifts and not our possessions. St John of the Cross wrote: 'Does it make any difference whether a bird be held by a slender thread or a rope? While the bird is bound and cannot fly till the cord that holds it be broken?'[7] It is the petty things which sometimes bind us most, and the thin threads which refuse to let us go. It is little luxuries and foolish indulgences which become so often the very things which hinder us most in our journey. As C. S. Lewis wrote (see p. 31). 'We are half-hearted creatures fooling about with drink and sex and ambition when infinite joy is offered us . . . like an ignorant child who wants to go on making mud pies in a slum because he cannot imagine what is meant by the offer of a holiday at the sea. We are far too easily pleased.'[8]

So in the end eternal life is not something we can go out and get – it is something, like everything else in life. It is a gift. All true life is charismatic, for that is what the word means – something which is given. Everything, from our daily bread to prayer and our next breath, is a gift from God. God is a prodigal and generous giver, yet only those who are really poor in spirit are in a position to receive His gifts and enjoy them for ever.

We begin to travel when we begin to see, and we saw how Bartimaeus stands like a signpost on the road for travellers with his prayer – 'Master, let me receive my sight.' We saw how we need to be able to see through things and beyond them, otherwise we turn our icons into idols and that will end up by breaking our hearts. It is these things which will rob us of joy – the very joy that it is their task to convey to us. But the joy is not to be found in them, it comes *through* them. So there is a time for embracing and there is another time for letting go, and we need to hear many times for ourselves the challenge of Jesus 'there is one thing you still lack'. If we let go now it will be easier than if we delay until tomorrow, and far easier than if we delay until next year: Holiness is always easier now!' (John Henry Newman). So the rich young man went away sorrowful. But make no mistake about it: although it would have been easier for him to 'let go' then, rather than later, God in Christ still looks on him and loves him. That is the constant – the terrifying constant. While we reject that love and its demand, it is hell on earth. While we hover and 'halt between two opinions' (1 Kings 18:21) with that love and its challenges it is purgatory –.on earth. But at those moments when we are

able to say yes – 'amen' – to that love and to all its demands;
then, for a second, that is heaven on earth.

He went away sorrowful. He turned round all right, but i
was in the wrong direction for he walked away from Jesus
So near and yet so far! We know the names of Bartimaeus
and Zacchaeus. They were nobodies who became some
bodies. But this man is anonymous – a nobody. He was
good man, but his very goodness had been the enemy of th
best. In order to get on to the right road he would have ha
to have turned round and seen everything upside down an
back to front. In a word, he would have had to have bee
converted. The terrible thing is that we can be travelling i
the right direction but facing the wrong way. Many goo
people are. It is as though we are being driven in a car wit
our backs to the engine. It's most uncomfortable. We rea
all the signs back-to-front, so that they do not make sens
and if we are not careful we shall end up by being car-sic
We need to face the right way and then we shall see thing
very differently. All things will be signs pointing us in th
direction of our journey. We shall be converted and ou
goodness will become holiness. Goodness is what a ma
has: holiness is what he is given. This young man was ric
in what he had, but he was sadly lacking in what he coul
receive. Poor man! – that's how Jesus saw him. He did no
see him as a rich man but as a poor man, and it made Jesu
sad because He loved him.

But it made the young man even more sad, for we are tol
that he went away full of sorrow. All that he had had robbe
him of what he could only be given. Little wonder that h
went away sorrowful.

> To turn aside from Thee is hell
> To walk with Thee is heaven.[9]

Prayer

O God, who hast prepared for them that love thee such good things as pass man's understanding; Pour into our hearts such love toward thee, that we, loving thee in all things and above all things, may obtain thy promises which exceed all that we can desire; through Jesus Christ our Lord. Amen.

(Collect for Sixth Sunday after Trinity, with medieval amendment.)

CHAPTER FOUR

THE WOMAN WITH THE ALABASTER FLASK OF OINTMENT:

FAILURE AND FORGIVENESS

One of the Pharisees asked him to eat with him, and he went into the Pharisee's house, and took his place at table. And behold, a woman of the city, who was a sinner, when she learned that he was at table in the Pharisee's house, brought an alabaster flask of ointment, and standing behind him at his feet, weeping, she began to wet his feet with her tears, and wiped them with the hair of her head, and kissed his feet, and anointed them with the ointment. Now when the Pharisee who had invited him saw it, he said to himself, 'If this man were a prophet, he would have known who and what sort of woman this is who is touching him, for she is a sinner.' And Jesus answering said to him, 'Simon, I have something to say to you.' And he answered, 'What is it, Teacher?' 'A certain creditor had two debtors; one owed five hundred denarii, and the other fifty. When they could not pay, he forgave them both. Now which of them will love him more?' Simon answered, 'The one, I suppose, to whom he forgave more.' And he said to him, 'You have judged rightly.' Then turning towards the woman he said to Simon, 'Do you see this woman? I entered your house, you gave me no water for my feet, but she has wet my feet with her tears and wiped them with her hair. You gave me no kiss, but from the time I came in she has not ceased to kiss my feet. You did not anoint my head with oil, but she has anointed my feet with ointment. Therefore I tell you, her sins, which are many, are forgiven, for she loved much; but he who is forgiven little, loves little.' And he said to her, 'Your sins are forgiven.' Then those who

*were at table with him began to say among themselves, 'Who
is this, who even forgives sins?' And he said to the woman,
'Your faith has saved you; go in peace.'*
   (Luke 7:36–50).

Truly, I say to you, wherever the gospel is preached in the
whole world, what she has done will be told in memory of
her' (Mark 14:9). So it should be, for it is the very heart of
the gospel and indeed in this story, in its various traditions
in the four gospels, is encapsulated the essential Gospel –
the good news of forgiveness.

The picture is unforgettable, because in many ways it is a
recurring picture and it rings true from start to finish.
Initially, it is an object lesson in prayer and worship. So
much of our praying is limited and sterile because we try to
conduct it mainly as an intellectual exercise which is
carried on two inches above the eyes! In fact and in
practice, true worship and prayer is an activity in which
we offer and present to God 'ourselves, our souls and
bodies'.[1] According to the words of St Paul, in true worship
we need to present our bodies (Romans 12:1). In practice, so
often, we try to leave them outside of church. Even worse
still, to try to inflict upon them postures which distract us
in worship. 'Prayer is not a matter of thinking a great deal
but of loving a great deal' (St Teresa of Avila). True prayer
should certainly seek to involve the body and not bypass it
or try to ignore it. True worship must involve all the senses,
and here is a woman who had given her body frequently and
knew what it meant to 'present' her body. She was in that
sense a sensual woman, and yet in many ways she is one of
the characters of the New Testament who can lead us best
to the threshold of worship. For now at last she had found
someone to whom she could give not only her body – but
herself, her soul and body as well. She knew as surely as
God knows that we cannot have a purely spiritual
relationship with anyone. God's relationship with us
includes Him saying to us: 'This is my Body which is given

for you.' In order for God to give Himself to man involved bodies: Mary's body at the annunciation; Christ' body broken on the cross; the evidence of His risen Bod ('Reach forward your hand . . .'); then His sacramenta body in the eucharist; and also the mystical body, men an women who by the same Holy Spirit are indeed His body i the world. We should be foolish indeed, if not blas phemous, to suppose that our response to God, earthboun bodies that we are, could ever bypass the flesh and blood o our own bodies and senses as a daily reminder of who w are and of all our relationships through the body. And s this woman is not ashamed to make her love, her praye and her worship of Christ an act of love in which her bod plays its part. But now it is to be as a truly sacramental ac This is the breakthrough for her. In the past, the outward visible and tangible carried no inward commitment. No the outward and visible carried with it all that she had t give of her inward and spiritual self. This was not simpl another occasion of 'ships passing in the night'. This was sacramental act of integrity – in which every respons was bent upon one purpose – love, the love of Go The fragmentation of sensuality was at last healed: not b suppressing it or rejecting it, but rather by the dis covery of someone worthy of a total offering of all that sh had and all that she was. Happy the man or woman wh finds that their Lord and their lover are one and the sam person!

But to the cautious this is a scandal and a cause of offenc It always has been and it always will be. Whenever, and i whatever form, worship and religion begin to demand total offering, the cautious stand by in criticism and even i horror, nearly always, strangely enough, whenever involves the body or the Body: the veneration of the cross i the liturgy of Good Friday or the first time Christ washe the disciples' feet. These are moments when the Churc seems to be going a bit too far – we call it extreme and w dub such people as extremists. We sometimes call it 'hig church' and that is another safe way of keeping it in an area in which it will not challenge us. It is the sense of total abandonment which makes people feel uncomfortable in just those very areas where they most need healing. So naturally enough the observers and the religious people who were sitting around and watching were scandalized.

They always have been and they always are. But notice just how wrongly they interpret it – surely enough, they got it the wrong way round. 'If this man were a prophet he would have known who and what sort of woman this is who is touching him.' They suppose that if God knows all He will not accept all: and so they are trapped, even in their religion, in trying to cover up and keep up outward appearances. Yet the truth is the very opposite from this. 'Jesus knew what was in man and needed no one to tell him' (John 2:25). It is precisely because Christ knows where we are most vulnerable, and because He knows all, that He is ready to forgive all. This woman, by instinct, had come to the experience of justification by God's grace which thousands of years of Pharisaical law had not achieved. It was precisely *because* Jesus knew what sort of woman it was who was touching Him that He accepted her love and worship. He needed no one to tell Him that – thank God! References – good or bad – are of no account in the presence of God and in our dealings with God, now or on the day of judgement.

It is this point which had brought the whole tremendous religious consciousness of the Jewish race – God's chosen people – to a halt in their religious development. The law was intended to be a 'tutor' to bring us to this very point, where we could receive grace and forgiveness (Galatians 3:24). Yet by a strange inversion – which is itself at the heart of all human tragedy – the very means to the end had become an end in itself. Sinful man – even religious sinful man – misses the point of it all once again. That is why good men – rather than blatant sinners – at the last moment can find it so hard to enter the kingdom of heaven. Their goodness – which is still not good enough – prevents them from reaching out to receive the best: nothing less than God Himself. Their good works, their religious obser-vances, which should bring them with joyful expectation to the very threshold of God's grace, become the very reason why they hold back in self-assurance and self-sufficiency. And so it is, that the religious and good people can be near to the kingdom of God by distance, even right outside the front door, yet if they are to enter, they have to turn right round in order to approach it and enter by another route altogether. We can be so near *by distance* and yet we can be so far away *by approach*.[2] The publicans and sinners who know that they cannot be self-sufficient – they have had their hearts broken too many times for that – they, it is, who perhaps by *distance* seem a long way from the kingdom of heaven and yet who are nevertheless those who, by *approach*, are facing the right way. They are nearer by route than so many who seem to spend their lives on the doorstep – hanging round the doorposts, not going in themselves, and preventing others from entering (Luke 11:52). So let us look more clearly at the picture of this story, until we know every detail by heart. For this is the picture we have here. She was 'weeping' and 'began to wet his feet with her tears'. There is something very catholic about tears. They often accompany the very great and deep moments in our life, and if von Hugel is right and religion is in fact 'the deepest of all experiences of the deepest of all facts' we should not be surprised frequently to find tears at the great turning points in our life. If this woman is Mary of Magdala – as in some traditions she is – she was also in tears at the moment of the resurrection in the garden, as surely as she was also at His feet in Simon's house and on Calvary hill, and both are scenes where we are deep into the reality of forgiveness and where tears are present.

Then again there were Peter's tears after his three-fold betrayal of Christ, and here again we are heavily into forgiveness and all that is implied by it. Once again there is the witness of tears. We are told that Peter went out and wept bitterly. But Judas just went out – and hanged himself. There is the difference between catholic forgiveness and the guilt of the zealot. And finally, as though all this evidence were not enough to permit us tears without shame (whether we are men or women), there is the most important evidence of all: 'Jesus wept' (John 11:35). We can thank God that, in the necessarily limited details we have of Christ in the gospel records, this fact is recorded, speaking volumes of reassurance where and when we need it most. We shall not travel far into the depth of catholic experience without tears. They can bring healing, peace and reconciliation in what spiritual writers have frequently called 'a baptism of tears'. They are part of a living and authentic tradition, and we ignore the release that they can bring at our peril.

Then we are told she was standing 'behind Him', because we must realize that she could not face Him, and, like the publican in the story of prayer in the temple, she could not even raise her eyes to look up (Luke 18:10). And yet it was the publican in that story who went away justified, rather than the Pharisee. And so it is here. The Pharisees – they sat facing Him. Yet who is nearest to Him by approach? The woman of course. She is on the road to forgiveness. She is facing in the right direction, but those who are facing Him in arrogance and self-assurance do not even know the meaning of the word forgiveness.

> And every human heart that breaks, in prison
>   cell or yard
> Is as that broken box that gave its treasure
>   to the Lord,
> And filled the unclean leper's house with scent of
>   costliest nard.[3]

She was broken already as surely as the alabaster jar of

ointment was broken, as surely as the body of our Lord was to be broken on the Cross, and as surely as, minute by minute, throughout the whole world, the priest breaks the bread at the altar at the eucharist. This is the raw material of redemption. The religious man or the good man, or even worse the self-sufficient man, must first be 'broken' before he can learn this way. It is essentially the way of the nails, which Thomas found from the outset and which had so fascinated him. It is the way by which our breakdowns can be offered to God and become opportunities of breakthrough. It is not our sins at the end of the day which need necessarily be the greatest hurdle in our pilgrimage; it is much more our refusal to accept forgiveness, to learn daily to live not in our own strength but in His, that will most likely keep us from the kingdom of heaven. This woman is nearer *by approach* to Paul's expression than the Pharisees *by distance* could ever be when St Paul wrote: 'God's strength is made perfect in man's weakness.' Saul, the Pharisee, was a thousand light years away from that understanding until on *his* pilgrimage he bumped into the frailty and vulnerability of Christ on the Damascus road, and then in that flash and blinding light he saw the point of it all and realized at last that the law was 'a tutor to bring us to Christ' (Galatians 3:24).

And so, in the story of St Luke, Christ tells the parable of the two debtors. How often we need to hear this story ourselves – not once, but 'seventy times seven' (Matthew 18:22). It is the route on our pilgrimage we need to know off by heart. We need to know every blade of grass at this turning point in the road if we are not to lose our way in justification by works, in anxious and self-righteous do-gooding, and if we are really to know that by myself I can do nothing, but in Christ 'I can do all things in him who strengthens me' (Philippians 4:13). Because the savage truth is that he who is forgiven little will love little, and he who is forgiven much will love much. This is the way of holiness, which is not quite the same way as the way of goodness. Yet this is God's way and not man's way. It is the way by which the catholic Church of Jesus is best recognized – the way of love which is the way of forgiveness. ('By this all men will know that you are my disciples, if you have love for one another' (John 13:35).) Yet what have we done with all this great treasure of the Gospel? Does the Church really communicate to the world that we are primarily a group of forgiven and forgiving sinners? We have rushed around promoting love parcelled up as good works. Yet the implications of Christ's equation of love and forgiveness, if properly understood, are almost devastating. The Church will be recognized for what it is because it loves much. It will love much because it has been forgiven much – the company of the forgiven. In other words, the catholic Church of Jesus Christ was made up of the sort of material which needs much forgiveness – like that early church in Corinth (viz. 1 Corinthians 1). The Church will be made up of the riff-raff of society, the broken and the sinful and the forgiven. They will be in a real sense God's holy, forgiven people. In the parable of the gospels it was the lame and the blind who were brought in to fill the feast, and not those who had originally received the invitation (Luke 14:16–24). We can safely leave the self-righteous and condemning world of goodness to those who have put their trust in such things, for we know that Christ came not to call the righteous but sinners to repentance. So we must never be shocked by sins as Christians. Jesus was never shocked by people's sins in the New Testament. He was much more shocked by their fear or their lack of faith. It is so sad when a priest or a leading layman is involved in some public scandal, and the press and the man in the street throw up their hands in horror and condemnation. Our modern, godless society is in fact very prudish in sudden and unexpected ways. The Church is just as much a hospital for sinners as it is a home for saints, and we should not be shocked when the lid is lifted on moral frailty, any more than we should be shocked when

we enter the casualty department of a large hospital. Man is
frail in every way, and the answer is not to throw up our
hands in horror but in a practical and matter-of-fact way to
seek to bring forgiveness and healing to bear in just those
places where it is most needed. The Christian attitude is
not to *throw up* one's hands but to *lay on* one's hands in love
and reconciliation and forgiveness. It takes a long time to
nail a man to a piece of wood, and so an accurate translation
of the first word from the Cross would imply that Jesus said
many, many times, 'Father forgive, Father forgive.'
Equally it takes a long time for a man or a woman to become
whole and really free from their sins. We need to hear many
times and on many occasions (seventy times seven is the
New Testament 'clue') 'Your sins are forgiven . . . go in
peace' (Luke 7:48 and 50).

But the more we are forgiven the more we shall love, and
it is love not moral rectitude by which Christ wishes us to
be recognized as His followers. It is one of the first
'catholic' signs that *all* men, we are told, will recognize
(John 13:35). Is this perhaps the reason why so much
political action and right social concern in the churches is
so unattractive, cold and moralistic, ready to condemn and
grudging to others? That would certainly be the case if it
arises from a church which has not first grasped and
experienced continually the place of failure and forgiveness, from which all true loving issues. A Pelagian church is
an ugly church – even if its deeds are more in the direction
of the love of neighbour than the love of God. A sinful
church can be a forgiven church, and a forgiven church will
be a loving church; a loving church will be a holy church
and it is that sort of church which will best express its
continuing love of and gratitude to God, by love and
concern for others. Indeed, at the end of the day, these are
not differing alternatives, for my love of my neighbour will
still be part of my primary love of God, who is in my
neighbour as surely as Christ is fed in the hungry, visited in
the sick and released in the captive. They can never be

alternatives. But we must get our priorities right. We shall love much if we are forgiven much.

All mainstream churches make provision for confession in one form or another. Some insist on it more than others. One of the wonderful breakthroughs of the charismatic movement has been the realization that all Christian pilgrims need to be ministered to in a personal way, which in its turn brings healing and new life. There will be few – if any – who will keep travelling on their pilgrimage without a turning point, or turning points, rather like the one which took place in Simon's house long ago. It is a story which will be told wherever the Gospel is told – but it is the Gospel precisely also because it is the story which countless men and women can tell of their own pilgrimages over two thousand years. A moment of breakdown – tears and release. A moment of truth and forgiveness, which in its turn brought the release of more love and deeper healing. For the Church is in business for salvation, and by derivation from the Latin (*salvus*) it means that the Church is in the health business. That is to say that we do not believe that all illness is the result of a straight equation with sin. Indeed, the New Testament turns its back on this over-simplification: 'Who sinned, this man or his parents?' 'Neither,' says Jesus (John 9:3f).

But we *do* know that wherever man is caught in his sins he is diseased, and therefore forgiveness brings healing, which is not necessarily the same as the curing of symptoms. Nevertheless there is an overlap between healing and forgiveness. 'Which is easier to say, thy sins are forgiven or take up thy bed and walk?' (Mark 2:9). The Christian is concerned with more than merely curing symptoms. Nine lepers were cured of leprosy but only one was healed (Luke 17:17). He was the one who turned round and came back to meet Jesus and so was *saved* (received salvation, i.e. health). It is a most happy sign in all the churches today that in obedience to the command of the epistle of St James in chapter five, personal forgiveness,

laying on of hands, anointing and prayer are a familiar
pattern of personal renewal, and mark for many the turning
point in the road on the way to resurrection, renewal and
fullness of life.

It is never too early and it is never too late for these kinds
of moments. You can leave it to the last minute – some do
like the thief on the cross. The only trouble is that the
longer you leave it the harder it is. But sooner or later, a
man or a woman comes to that point when they are finished,
broken down and defeated. It can be a blessed moment
indeed if it is the moment when God can begin, when God
can break through and when we can be raised up in the
strength of Christ's victory and not by pulling ourselves up
by our own shoestrings. Such a moment – or such moments
– become part of our own personal record and we should
not be ashamed to relate this story whenever and wherever
we are trying to explain the Gospel to others – for it is
essentially our Gospel. 'I will tell you what the Lord has
done for my soul.' It is the essential turning point which
turns a man or a woman round to see the face of Jesus, as
surely as Peter saw Him after his denial in the courtroom,
and as surely as Mary turned round in the garden of the
resurrection when she heard her name on the lips of her
Lord and so fell on her face, embracing His body with tears
and love. Many would have regarded Mary of Magdala as
the end! She was! But the forgiven Mary represents for all
of us the divine reversal – the last which had become first.
So she, the forgiven sinner, is first to witness the risen
Christ. In the gospel record and wherever that gospel is
told throughout the world she is not the last – on the
contrary, she is the first because she was forgiven much and
she loved much.

Prayer

Jesu, what didst thou find in me,
That thou hast dealt so lovingly?
All that I am or have is thine,
And thou, sweet Saviour, thou art mine.
Jesu, my Lord, I thee adore,
O make me love thee more and more.[5]

CHAPTER FIVE

THE GOOD MAN OF THE HOUSE:
WORSHIP AND GENEROSITY

And on the first day of Unleavened Bread, when they sacrificed the passover lamb, his disciples said to him, 'Where will you have us go and prepare for you to eat the passover?' And he sent two of his disciples, and said to them, 'Go into the city, and a man carrying a jar of water will meet you; follow him, and wherever he enters, say to the householder, "The Teacher says, Where is my guest room, where I am to eat the passover with my disciples?" And he will show you a large upper room furnished and ready; there prepare for us.' And the disciples set out and went to the city, and found it as he had told them; and they prepared the passover.

(Mark 14:12–16)

'The good man of the house' – who on earth was he anyway? We have no written account in the New Testament of a meeting between him and Jesus. However, it is clear from what is handed down to us that he knew of Jesus, and that at some point he must have met Him. What is even more important is that Jesus knew him and Jesus trusted him. No, we have no name for this man and we have not really many clues as to who he might have been. However, his name is written in heaven and we shall see why. According to three of the gospels, Jesus asked for a room where He might celebrate the Passover with His disciples. And so as part of the security and subterfuge of the days leading immediately up to the arrest of Jesus, we are told that the Master sent the disciples into the city, to follow a man carrying a pitcher of water and to ask him for a guest room (Greek *katalyma*) where the Passover might be celebrated. 'The good man of the house' would show them a large upper room furnished (Greek *aliyah*). The point which here deserves our reflection is the fact that Jesus only asked for *katalyma* and was in fact offered *aliyah*. If we translate these words correctly we shall realize that Jesus asked for the smallest room in the house (a guest room): the sort of place where, according to one commentary, in a large English house you would keep the deck chairs, the croquet mallets and the tennis rackets! In fact, however, Jesus was offered the largest and the best room in the house ('a large upper room furnished'). The good man of the house was asked for the least and he gave the largest: he was asked for the smallest and he gave the best. He was and he is the good man of the Lord's house – he is a sign of the good layman of the Church.

But it's worth pressing on with our meditation – even if we can be accused of cheating a little. Tradition has it that the 'upper room' was in John Mark's mother's house, and it would not be wholly dishonest to connect this 'upper room' with the upper room where the disciples were assembled, behind locked doors for fear of the Jews, on the first day of the week when the risen Christ appeared to them (viz. John 21). Furthermore, it may well have been the same 'upper room' where they waited, all together in one place, when the Spirit was given at Pentecost and where the Church was born two thousand years ago. So, just stop to think. That good man in his generosity gave the best possible room in his house. It may well be that he moved out of it himself and held his own Passover ceremonies in a more modest room while Jesus was given the best in the house. And yet it was in that 'upper room' that the eucharist of the Christian Church was initiated, the risen Christ appeared, the Holy Spirit was given and that is where it all began. And equally that is where it so often all begins – with worship and generosity.

For generosity is the very nature of God Himself. We

hear much talk today of stewardship of the resources of the
universe – and rightly so. But alongside the concept of the
careful and responsible stewardship of these resources, in
the Bible it is necessary to place the complementary truth of
the prodigality of God. God is a big giver. In his famous
hymn 'Praise to the Holiest in the height' Newman has the
two parallel verses 'O wisest Love' and then a verse or two
later 'O *generous* Love'. In nature and in the universe
around us we see much evidence of God's generosity. We
would need only the guest room of a small world to live out
our redemption if we saw it only in functional terms, but in
fact God Himself shows us a large and vast universe
generously furnished, in which the oblation of our
redemption was offered and in which it continues to be
offered. 'Small is beautiful' but at the same time big is
generous and both are aspects of God's nature. So His
command to us follows not from common sense but from
revelation: 'If anyone forces you to go one mile, go with
him two miles' (Matthew 5:41). Likewise, 'If any one
would sue you and take your coat, let him have your cloak
as well' (Matthew 5:40). The picture is the same throughout the whole of the New Testament, whether it be in the
synoptic gospels where we see the 'good measure of grain'
'pressed down' and running over (Luke 6:38); or whether
we look to the first sign in Cana of Galilee where it is the
water pots 'filled up to the brim' (John 2:7). The witness of
all four traditions is consistent – generosity in loving. The
good man of the house was most godlike in his generosity.
But stop to think what God can do with that sort of
generous oblation. It is the raw material for the real
presence of Christ Himself by the work of the Holy Spirit;
it is a veritable Pentecost forming the Church (the mystical
Body of Christ) again by the overshadowing of the Holy
Spirit. 'Where charity and love are, there is God, there is
God.' It is not too much of an exaggeration to say that the
Church is, and the Body of Christ is, formed most
conspicuously by the overshadowing of the Holy Spirit

upon the oblation and offering of generous worship.

For the work of our redemption is never spiritual, it involves our offering as well as God's revelation, in order for Christ to be truly present. So often in history we have allowed the emphasis to fall in one way or the other: a spiritual church which is totally the sovereignty of God at work on the one hand, or a self-made Pelagian church which is the result of man's strivings and efforts on the other hand. But in a true understanding of God's saving work, God invites us to respond with our offering and it is these offerings which He can take, bless, break and give – it is these offerings which are consecrated and transformed to become the Body of Christ. We are indeed as St Paul reminds us, fellow workers together with God (2 Corinthians 6:1); or in the perfect balance as set out by St Augustine of Hippo: 'Without him we cannot: without us he will not.'

'Without us he will not.' The world waits for the blessed Virgin Mary to say *Fiat mihi* – Amen or just O.K.! That is necessary, because without her flesh and blood the offering would not be complete and Christ would not be formed in our midst. God in Christ never crushes us by His generosity: on the contrary, He invokes our generosity and love through His initiative: 'We love, because he first loved us' (1 John 4:19). All Christian effort is rooted first in our experience of God's stunning generosity. He invites us to offer what we have in response to His need. God has no need in Himself for Himself: but in us and for us He needs our co-operation. So the woman at the well is ironically asked to draw water for the one who is Himself the well of Life (John 4). The man (possibly the same good man of the house) is asked for an ass for the Palm Sunday procession by the one who could call for 'twelve legions of angels' (Matthew 26:53). In the words of the gospel, 'Tell him that the Lord has need of them' (Matthew 21:3). Our redemption was not achieved by a divine fiat and then handed on with a memorandum circulating the universe. It is a continual and continuing process of God's costly generous self-giving, inviting us to respond with similar offerings of generous love.

So we must not indulge in cheap grace. 'I will not offer to the Lord that which costs me nothing' (2 Samuel 24:24) was King David's response to the offer of a free-for-nothing threshing floor where he might build a temporary altar for the Lord. Only the best for God. 'Love so amazing, so divine, demands my soul, my life, my all.'[1] Small change has no place in God's work – unless it is the small coin which is the total offering of everything that we have and everything that we are, as in the case of the widow with her mite (Mark 12:42).

The Church of God was founded in a large upper room furnished, which represented the best which anybody could give and of the best that the good man had to offer. Who knows, it might well have been his personal thank-offering to Jesus for some miracle of healing to a daughter, a son, a friend or a relative. What is certain is that the Church will only survive where there are good men and women willing to give to God's work generously and costingly. Our collections and church offerings are not there to pay the bills – that is secondary and irrelevant. They are primarily there as thank offerings to God, in order that we may have the opportunity to co-operate with God in Christ in furthering the work of the cenacle of the whole Christian Church – namely a place for the Body of Christ (sacramental and mystical) to be found wherever the Holy Spirit overshadows offerings which have been made from a generous heart. It is worth reflecting that the good man of the house still had to find somewhere else where he and his family could celebrate their Passover – possibly in the small guest room! He had given up the best to God and kept the small change for himself. How seldom that is the case. Usually it is the other way round: I keep the best for myself and give the second best and leftovers, together with the small change, for the work of God in His Church.

There are some today who purvey a dangerous half-truth and would assert that the Church does not need buildings. Of course, it goes without saying that the Church is not primarily a building. On the contrary, it is people, and the Church is what is left when the building has been burnt to the ground. Furthermore, in times of persecution and indeed in days when we need to look to our priorities, no one would pretend that we cannot learn a very great deal from *being* the Church, and from meeting in homes and other places without the overheads and costs of large buildings and too many of them at that.

But nevertheless, while we are creatures of time and space we need to learn to know God somewhere if we are going to be able to recognize Him everywhere. Of course He is everywhere, but if we set out by trying to know Him everywhere we shall end up by knowing Him nowhere. We are called to love everybody, but the best way to begin is by trying to love somebody, otherwise we might end up by loving nobody. (I have never forgotten a poster with the words 'I love mankind – it's just people I don't like!') We affirm the general by locating the particular and so with churches and shrines. We need holy places, places set apart for God *somewhere* if we are to come to know Him and love Him *everywhere*. Furthermore, Christianity at its best has never claimed to be a spiritual religion but an incarnate religion, caught up with – or better still – catching up and lifting up the ordinary bricks and mortar, pounds and pence, people and places of everyday life and giving them a significance and presence beyond the ordinary. There is a right place for the love of a building, a shrine, a holy place, where we come to know and to love the living God. There is a place and there is a time to sing:

These stones that have echoed their praises
    are holy
And dear is the ground where their feet once
    have trod.[2]

Of course when there comes a moment to decide between outward and visible and inward and spiritual, it is the latter which must claim our first allegiance. The 'cat' Christian is more concerned for the furnishings and fittings, the comfort of the sofa, and sits lightly to the presence of the master. The 'dog' Christian enjoys the household of faith with all that it can offer, but he will follow the master when the time to move arrives, even if the conditions are primitive and the decor somewhat severe!

And all this because the new creation – from the Body of Christ – will not be spiritual and abstract but will be a fusion of the kingdoms of this world and the 'kingdom of our Christ and his God' (Revelation 11:15). It will be a due of God and man, spirit and matter, heaven and earth, which by the brooding and overshadowing of the Holy Spirit will become the new creation – the Body of Christ. That is a more wonderful experiment in generosity than the first creation. Indeed, probably more wonderful than a thousand million other creations which represent only God's work – places for angels and archangels. But saints are made of sterner stuff. The frailty of our personality with all its limitations, combining with the limitless and infinite resources of God – that is the greatest experiment of all.

With the end product of that co-operation we have something which transcends both heaven and earth – namely the Body of Christ.

So worship and oblation are the way *through*: they are supremely the route to resurrection. Man is a compulsive worshipper and needs to worship, but he needs to find someone or something worthy of his worship. 'Why was I created?' asks the Scottish catechism. 'In order to worship God and to enjoy him for ever', or as the psychiatrist says in the play *Equus*: 'If you don't worship, you will shrink: it's as brutal as that.'[3] Worship is the way of losing self in obedience to Christ's injunction that unless a man loses his life he cannot find it (Mark 8:35).

Man the marvel seeing
Forgets his selfish being
For joy of the beauty not his own.[4]

Of course that sort of worship is excessive and demanding and costly, but it is the most essentially human activity without which man is locked and limited within the confines of his own parochial horizons. Worship is in many ways the most authentic witness, for it points to God for God's own sake, and refuses to trivialize Him and make Him simply a convenient projection of man's need for fulfilment. There is much talk in the Church at the present time of the fulfilment of prayer and the fulfilment of worship. That is only secondary and a by-product of the fact that true worship springs from a grateful and thankful heart, which is lost in adoration and praise and which points to God for God's own sake.

It was this sheer worship of God for God's own sake which captivated Professor Joad, who for a large part of his life professed a militant atheism. When, towards the end of his life, he was shown round Lincoln Cathedral by the Dean, he was eventually taken right up into the triforium where the Dean, in a moment of unselfconscious demonstration, said that he would like to show the Professor what was sometimes regarded as one of the finest carvings in the whole building. It was, however, tucked away in the roof. 'It must have been done for the glory of God,' said the Dean as a throw-away line, 'since no one else could probably have been expected to see it!' It was that offering – 'the cream of all my heart'[5] – done to the glory of God, which broke through years of intellectual argument for Professor Joad and witnessed most convincingly to the existence of God – a God who *is,* whether we like it or not, and a God who *is there,* whether we believe in Him or not.

The good man of the house, by offering the best he had to give, set Christian witness in the environment of worship, and in doing so began a whole continuing tradition which

over two thousand years has continually recalled the
presence of Christ in the sanctuary of the hearts of all who
have loved Him. The good man of the house stands for all
those who, over two thousand years, have offered the very
best they had to give: musicians and artists; painters and
sculptors; brass cleaners and flower arrangers, and all who
have helped to prepare and condition the 'large upper
room' ready for the service of worship and offering. Of
course there is always a danger that it can stop there, and of
course it will if it is ever done for reasons of self-
justification or in the naïvely blasphemous view that we can
buy love. True lovers know that you cannot buy love, yet
true lovers have always wanted to give presents and gifts
and outward, tangible tokens of their love and gratitude.
Here, as in so many places, there is a danger of getting
things the wrong way round. Love expresses itself in gifts,
but gifts can never buy love or earn it. Love is a free and
undeserved gift and that is the way God loves it to be. But
we in our turn thank God and give Him praise, worship and
thanksgiving by our free-will offering of everything to
Him. At the end of the day it is not too much to say that we
can see all life as a gift. The scriptures speak of the whole
Church as the gift of the Father to the Son. Right at the
heart of God, there is an oblation, offering, giving and
receiving in love. We get very near to the heart of God,
and indeed very near to the heart of the whole matter, when
we offer the 'cream of all our heart' as a thank offering to
God.

For it should go without saying, that at the end of the day
there is nothing we can give God that He needs or wants
more than the gift of ourselves and our hearts. It is that
sanctuary of the heart for which God is most jealous. But in
a sacramental world that would show itself best in outward,
visible and tangible forms. 'No, not the guest room, but
only the best for the best: prepare the best room in the
house: the large one – the upper room, well furnished.'
Little did the good man of the house realize – or perhaps he

did – that in that room there would be a little bit of heaven on earth until such time as there was a lot of earth in the large upper room of heaven.

Prayer

Thanks be to thee, my Lord Jesus Christ,
For all the benefits which thou hast given me,
For all the pains and insults which thou hast borne
    for me.
O most merciful Redeemer, Friend and Brother,
May I know thee more clearly,
    love thee more dearly,
    follow thee more nearly. Amen.

                St Richard of Chichester

CHAPTER SIX

PETER:

VOCATION, WITNESS AND SERVICE

*When they had finished breakfast, Jesus said to Simon Peter,
'Simon, son of John, do you love me more than these?' He
said to him, 'Yes, Lord; you know that I love you.' He said
to him, 'Feed my lambs.' A second time he said to him,
'Simon, son of John, do you love me?' He said to him, 'Yes,
Lord; you know that I love you.' He said to him, 'Tend my
sheep.' He said to him the third time, 'Simon, son of John, do
you love me?' Peter was grieved because he said to him the
third time, 'Do you love me?' And he said to him, 'Lord, you
know everything; you know that I love you.' Jesus said to
him, 'Feed my sheep. Truly, truly, I say to you, when you
were young, you girded yourself and walked where you
would; but when you are old, you will stretch out your hands,
and another will gird you and carry you where you do not
wish to go.' (This he said to show by what death he was to
glorify God.) And after this he said to him, 'Follow me.'
Peter turned and saw following them the disciple whom Jesus
loved, who had lain close to his breast at the supper and had
said, 'Lord, who is it that is going to betray you?' When
Peter saw him, he said to Jesus, 'Lord, what about this man?'
Jesus said to him, 'If it is my will that he remain until I come,
what is that to you? Follow me!'* (John 21:15–22)

So it ends where it began – 'In my end is my beginning.'¹
'Follow me', that's how it had all begun. It seems a long
time now since Peter had first heard those words back in the
balmy days of the early enthusiasms of Galilee. But a lot of
water had flowed under the bridge since then. Although

Palestine is a small country (not even the size of Wales), they had travelled a long way in every respect since those early days. It had seemed so straightforward then: now it was hopelessly complicated. 'Follow me.' 'But of course we will follow you – we will leave all to follow you – and we will go through death if need be.' But then when the pressures were on, and the crises came in the heady politics of Jerusalem, when matters of Church and State loomed large, it was not so easy to see where it was all leading. Furthermore, there had been the personal catastrophe of Peter's own personal denial and betrayal: 'while he was warming himself' (Mark 14:54). It had all happened in a flash. It was not a contrived or foreseen disaster: it was almost as though Peter had lost control of events. But Peter, the first to confess Christ at Caesarea Philippi, was now the last person to stand by Him when it came to the crunch at Jerusalem. 'Thou art the Christ' (Mark 8:29) – 'I do not even know the man you are talking about' (Mark 14:71). So, was that in fact where it was all going to end? Perhaps in spite of everything – resurrection and all – they had reached the parting of the ways. What was certain is that in any future plans, Peter could now have no part.

And so let's get back to fishing! (Simon Peter had said to them, 'I am going fishing' (John 21:3).) Yes, you can do what you like but I am going back to fishing. But it was still night: they caught nothing. Then 'just as day was breaking, Jesus stood on the beach'. Peter was really still in the dark. The resurrection had happened but it had not really yet happened for Peter. It had not yet 'dawned' on him what this was all about, what resurrection would mean for Peter. You see, Peter, you had thought that it was going to be so straightforward, the Lord's service. You had given up everything and surely this was just the kind of service of witness which the Lord needed if the kingdom was to come. In many ways you had a lot to offer.

Rise up, O men of God,
The church for you doth wait.
Her strength unequal to her task:
Rise up, and make her great.[2]

In so many ways, Peter, you had been the leader – the first in every way, and now you are the last. It's all over, so why not go back, turn round and return to fishing?

Here is for Peter, as for so many, the great hurdle in their pilgrimage. They have in one sense a lot to offer: but fulfilment will not come about that way. Being an apostle is not the same as setting out to put the world right. The Lord does not want zealots, not even servants; he wants, first and foremost, friends (viz. John 15:15). This kingdom is not going to be a kingdom built on an ideology. The world has had plenty of those, and each civilization has been left with only the dust of monuments and ancient ruins as a witness to their lasting validity. No, this kingdom is to be a *philadelphia* – a communion of friends. Therefore there will be no room in that sort of community just for proving yourself. The first step will be to know you are loved; then, and then only, can we go out to love others.

'So, Simon, son of Jonah, do you love me more than these?' It is all too clear that Jesus is speaking to the old man – the former man – for that had been Peter's name in the early days: Simon; even worse 'Simon, son of Jonah'. You can see jonahs flying all round the Sea of Galilee. They are fluttering doves – or at least that is one translation. So Simon, son of a fluttering dove! Still the old wayward, impetuous, unreliable Simon, son of a fluttering dove. But then, what can you expect? The leopard does not change his spots. But as though it were not enough to recall Simon's former nature by recalling him to his first name, Jesus asks 'Do you love me more than these?' Could it be, at that moment, that Peter's mind flashed back to the house of Simon the Pharisee, to the woman with the alabaster box of ointment? If so, then, those will love best who are forgiven most. To love Jesus more than others is to be in need of His forgiveness more than others. Our love will not be based on our capacity for goodness or service: rather it will be related directly to His great love of us and our great need of His continuing forgiveness. There is no room in the kingdom for that loveless, self-righteous service which sets out to love others as a compensation for our own inadequacies and even self-hatred. We must first come to the saving knowledge of God's love for us, before we can go out to others with the love with which we have been loved. It was Isaiah of old who only heard the call to service after he had first been forgiven and healed.

That is always the right order in this journey of maturity: vision, repentance, sacrifice, forgiveness, worship and vocation. Simon the disciple can only become Peter the apostle and the rock when he knows he is loved, and when he knows God's love in that very area where he has fallen hardest. Then, and then only, is the sky the limit. The Bible bids us love our neighbour as ourself: neither more nor less. So true service of others is related to true love of self. In the end (*in extremis*) there is only one who can love us with such totality: it is the one who knows all, and who has forgiven all. We need to know and to hear for ourselves, at some precious moment, that we are loved and that we are lovable. Good parents can go a long way in this process and good friends can later take up the refrain. But in so far as we all have a hidden side to ourselves, known only to God, it is only from God that the ultimate word of release can come. 'My song is love unknown; my Saviour's love for me.'

Sanctification, then, and vocation belong together and each needs the other. As I grow closer to God and love Him more I shall be able to love others better; but as I come to love others better I shall be loving God within them, and it will also be in and through them that I shall be loving God. The worship of the Church and the service of the world are not alternatives: they are inextricably bound together. There is not a Gospel and a Social Gospel: there is only one

Gospel – and it is inevitably a Social Gospel.

So this call to follow Jesus was to mean more than it had meant before, back in the early days in Galilee. That was only the echo. This was, and is, where the note was struck. Peter, you are to follow Him, not with strident self-confidence, but rather you are to follow Him and become like Him in His death and resurrection. His death was not some strange and unfortunate accident of circumstances. It was inevitable. That is what love in a frail and fallen world is all about. Likewise, the resurrection is not just a happy ending to an unpleasant story. It is what God can do and will always do with defeated humanity, when it turns in weakness and defeat to God's strength and Christ's victory. Peter, this is the pattern of true life. All else is bravado. The resurrection, Peter, is for you and in you. 'Follow me' was not an invitation to join a course: it was a question of going where He went, of undergoing what He underwent and overcoming through what He overcame. At the outset Peter had been the most vocal of the disciples in refuting the way of the Cross. It is important to notice how each resurrection appearance is specially tailored and turned, so that each disciple may come to know the power of Christ's resurrection in just that special and personal way in which they most need to know it. For Mary, it was still to do with the body: she must not cling to this body, but let go, because there is something more wonderful than this – the glorified body. Then there was Thomas – obsessed with 'the way' in which it was all to work out, and marked with the impression of the nails and wounds on Calvary hill. For him it was to be the realization that the wounds and the scars do not disappear, but that they are 'the way' to perfect love – 'the way' of the nails. The scars are transfigured: that is always 'the way' it will be. The scars of love become the essential features of the resurrection. So for Peter: he had to face this cross and not just try to get round it or get over it – he had to go *through* it until *he* could say 'In the Cross of Christ I glory, towering o'er the wrecks of time'.[3] The

Cross had been to him both a scandal and a foolishness, but now he must face up to it and see it for what it is – *the* way of salvation. The gibbet has become the throne: the scandal has become true glory. We see that Peter has learned this lesson in the first miracle recorded at his hands in the book of the Acts of the Apostles, when he says, 'Men of Israel, why do you wonder at this, or why do you stare at us, as though by our own power or piety we had made him walk?' (Acts 3:12). What a different Peter! Here is Peter living and working not in his own strength but in the power and strength of Christ's resurrection, so that indeed it is true and will be true of his ministry: 'Greater works than these shall you do' (John 14:12).

But thank God, Peter, you will no longer be your own man in all this. Now you are a bound man. 'When you were young, you bound yourself and walked where you wanted: but when you are old, you will stretch out your hands, and another will bind you and carry you where you do not wish to go' (John 21:18). Yes, the apostle is a bound man. There are in the Greek New Testament two words for servant or slave: *diakonos* and *doulos*. Our service for the world must always be a service and not a slavery. We are slaves of God in order to be servants of the world. But God help the man or woman who has become bound to the world – even in its needs and even in the name of service – unless they are first the slaves of God! If we become slaves of the world, we shall be joyless and so will those whom we are seeking to serve. Rather we must be slaves of God, set free from self, to serve the true needs of the world. That is the heart and shape of true apostolic service.

For freedom is not our birthright. Man is not born free, in the sense of being free to do anything. Iris Murdoch is right: 'we all have degrees of freedom' in different areas of our lives. They are not in practice very large areas of freedom. In fact man is highly predictable. 'Only Jesus was free not to sin,' says St Augustine. Even my virtues are frequently part of my obsessions, and if there are some sins that I do not commit it is probably because I am the sort of person who would not even be free to commit this sort of sin! I am not free to sin, so even my 'virtues' do not really belong to my freedom: they are part of my predictable limitations.

So mercifully, those who best serve God in the world are those who have at some stage in their pilgrimage come to this point of surrender. Bound to God, and so free from the paralysis of a supermarket of choices, they are in a real sense bound in order to be free. Free, then, for all – for ever, and for everywhere. God alone knows where that sort of freedom will end – almost the last place on earth we would ever have chosen! Bishop Wilson, the saintly Bishop of Birmingham, was for many years Bishop of Singapore, and during the Second World War he was tortured by the Japanese in a prisoner-of-war camp. But when he returned to England, and later became Bishop of Birmingham, he used to tell how, on the eve of his ordination, he had said to God that he would go anywhere in the world – well, anywhere that is except 'the Equator, the North Pole or Birmingham'! He loved to relate how at the age of seventy, after a ministry on the Equator and then as Bishop of Birmingham, he was now waiting for a call to the North Pole!

We do not know where such discipleship will end up, but we know how we shall end up. We shall end up with our little world turned upside down. It was to be Peter's actual experience to be crucified with Christ upside down. In some sense that is true for all Christians who follow Him in one way or the other. In some sense, known perhaps only to God, true discipleship turns our world upside down, and in some sense, known again perhaps only to God, we also are crucified with Christ. If we really witness to true love in a frail and fallen world, we shall suffer. It is no accident that the word martyr comes from a Greek word which means 'to witness'. There is no real witness to true love without suffering: but the reverse is not necessarily true, and we must never be a Church which cultivates martyrdom. What we can say is, as Christ teaches us, 'beware when all men speak well of you' (Luke 6:26). The Church must really be on the lookout if it becomes popular and seems to fit quite happily into the world around it. There is almost certainly something very fundamentally wrong with such a Church. Jesus never promised a comfortable ride to His followers, and right at the outset, when He had spoken with His disciples about their discipleship, He had spoken clearly about taking up the cross and following 'in the Way'. Peter had heard Him in those early days, but he had not really taken it in after all. But now, standing with Jesus at the crossroads, he sees the road stretching out ahead of him, with the shadow of the Cross over it. He had perhaps thought that all that sort of thing was behind him, and that the Cross was Calvary as a one-off event in the past – and in one sense it was. In one sense there was to be no going through all that again. Yet in another sense, it was still all in front of him, though at least this time he would know where it was all leading and the ultimate shape of things to come. 'What He has done for us must be done in us' (St Anselm).

But for a moment – yes, another moment – he lost his nerve. 'Peter turned . . .' (John 21:20). He turned round and looked over his shoulder and there was John – the closest human friend Jesus had ever had. In quite a special way John had always been closest to Jesus, as he was on the night of the Last Supper, close – very close – laying 'close to his breast'. He had stayed close to Jesus on Calvary – right to the bitter end, when he had taken care of Mary the mother of Jesus. In some special way they were like mother and son. For John it had turned out all right really. 'And so, Lord, what about your blue-eyed boy?'

There is here a real moment of anger and even resentment. Often when we receive our vocation we are angry with God and resentful that our road seems so hard compared with that of others. We compare and contrast our

way with theirs – those others who seem to have it all on
such a straightforward way. Yet, in the life of the body
there is no room for competition of the wrong kind. If one
member suffers the whole body suffers: if one member is
honoured the whole body is honoured (1 Corinthians
12:26). Another man's way is not mine, and my way will be
different from others. Christ, in His great mercy, gives to
all of us a way which will both meet our particular strengths
as well as our weaknesses, and He will not suffer us to be
tempted above that which we are able (1 Corinthians
10:13). Another man's way is not mine: I must learn to
follow Him.

'Peter turned . . .' Legend has it that, much further on the
road, Peter again lost his nerve and fled from Rome during
the Neronian persecution. On the road out of Rome he
heard the voice and the question: *Quo vadis?* Finally, Peter
turned round and went back to Rome, to suffer, to die, to
rise and to reign.

The turning points in our lives are many, and conversion
is seldom a once-for-all affair. Each moment of new
surrender opens us to further opportunities of growth and
commitment. Christ meets us at each of these moments
and the gospel word at each point is essentially the same –
'Follow me'. Peter had nearly thrown it all up and gone
back home to fishing, nets and boats and the straightforward life. In fact he never went home in that sense again.
He turned round and carried on travelling. He had, as
Christ had prayed, *turned again* and could now 'strengthen'
his brethren (Luke 22:31). From that turning point
onwards, he would be a displaced person, homesick for
heaven. Simon, son of Jonah (the unpredictable and even
unreliable fluttering dove), was at last to become, by God's
grace – but by God's grace alone – Peter the rock man, the
prince of the apostles. That is always the raw material on
which God's grace can best work: our frailties witness best
to His strengths: our fluttering inconsistencies show best
His rock-like steadfastness: our wavering and back-sliding

are the very turns in the road where we are most conscious
of His love and His infinite patience.

Prayer

Eternal God,
> the light of the minds that know thee,
> the joy of the hearts that love thee,
> the strength of the wills that serve thee;
Grant us so to know thee that we may truly love thee,
> so to love thee that we may freely serve thee,
> to the glory of thy holy name. Amen.

Gelasian

EPILOGUE

EPILOGUE

While they were talking and discussing together, Jesus
drew near and went with them.

Luke 24:15

Events in the New Testament prove nothing in themselves,
yet a substantial part of this book has given time to
meditating in some detail on the stories of five people who
met Jesus of Nazareth at a turning point in their lives.
These encounters made a deep impact and impression
upon them. Then we looked at Peter's meeting with Jesus
after the resurrection. Yet this encounter still belongs to
some extent in the same category as the others since Peter
had known Jesus 'in the flesh', and in one sense even this
post-resurrection encounter is heavily endowed with
expectations arising from a long and deep friendship with
Jesus of Nazareth, which predated the events of the
crucifixion. There can be little doubt that there was a man
called Jesus of Nazareth, and that He made a great
impression on those whom He met. Nevertheless, if that
had been where it had all ended – with the back cover of the
New Testament – then Christianity would today be little
more than an esoteric study of a first-century religious
movement which could only be of interest to scholars and
those who 'specialize' in such matters.

But the other half of the story which demands our
attention must surely be the existence of Christianity in the
world over the past two thousand years. For us, living in
the world today, the primary question which demands
meditation must surely be: 'Who are all these?' (Revelation
7:13). What about the millions and millions of men and

women – good, bad and indifferent – who, over the past two thousand years, have not been ashamed to be called Christians? So often we ask the wrong questions in the wrong order. We start by looking at the New Testament account in the gospels and saying: 'How could it all have happened?' But the most important question is, 'Why is it still happening today, and why is there still a Church two thousand years later?' We could of course write off the Church as a particular aspect of Western culture, perhaps in the Middle Ages, or we might even want to see it later on as a nineteenth-century aspect of 'the Tory party at prayer'. But a world view of Christianity in the 1980s, with the opening up of China revealing a living underground Church; the living Church in Russia and the Soviet Bloc after years of oppression; the power of Christianity in the emerging nations of Africa; and the huge growth in membership of the Christian Church in South America – that's a very different question, and it demands a very different answer. Try putting all that together in the same bundle of your imagination and you are simply bound to ask again and again, 'But who are all these?'

It was the existence of the Church as a contemporary fact which was for me the prime question when I was grappling with faith as an undergraduate, not least because I was studying history and knew all too well how passing movements had their little day, only eventually to disappear 'with a whimper', as though they had never been, never again to see the light of day except at the hands of some research student looking through dusty manuscripts in the British Museum. Surely, that is where you would expect to find the records of the passages we have been studying, instead of in copies of the most 'popular' book in the whole world? The problem, however, is primarily a problem about people and only secondarily a problem about a book. Gamaliel was right on target with his question: 'Before these days, Theudas arose giving himself out to be somebody, and a number of men, about four hundred, joined him; but he was slain and all who followed him were dispersed and came to nothing. After him, Judas the Galilean arose in the days of the census and drew away some people after him: he also perished, and all who followed him were scattered. So in the present case [Christianity] I tell you, keep away from these men and let them alone; for if this plan or this undertaking is of men it will fail: but if it is of God, you will not be able to overthrow them' (Acts 5:35–9).

The argument was powerful then in those first five minutes of Christianity. It is even more powerful today, two thousand years later. Only a scholar will be able to tell you who on earth Theudas was and what he said and did; or Judas the Galilean – whoever he might have been. But this Jesus of Nazareth is still on the streets of the world, He still has a following (in fact the largest crowd ever recorded in the history of the human race was recently convened in His name), and even the name itself draws the best box office takings in the longest-running musical ever known in London's West End. The very least that a pragmatic cool-headed Gamaliel would be compelled to conclude from the twentieth-century viewpoint, is that it is not another one of many movements which can be written off as enthusiastic 'undertakings' of men. At the very least this is of God.

For the truth is that ever since New Testament times men and women have been meeting the same Jesus at turning points in their lives, and have not been ashamed to testify to the difference which that encounter or those encounters have made to them. In fact it has made all the difference in the world. Of course, in a worldwide movement like Christianity, it takes all sorts to make up the Church – good, bad and indifferent – but nevertheless the hard core of truth remains. Men and women (too many to number and most of them unknown by name in the history books) have 'bumped' into this living Jesus – the risen Christ – on the road of life. They have been turned round by Him and had their outlook changed by Him. They would claim to have been forgiven and healed by Him. They have sacrificed much for Him and many of them have given their lives in service to others in His name, while equally many others over the years have laid down their own lives in martyrdom. What we have been studying in the pages of the New Testament is no once-for-all, dead archaeological record. It is a living book and what life is really all about – or, to borrow a phrase, 'this is your life!'

While they were talking and discussing together, Jesus drew near and went with them. The risen Christ is no longer restricted to Jericho, Galilee or Jerusalem: you meet Him on the road of life under many guises – while you are 'talking and discussing together'. He is frequently not recognized for who He is, but wherever we are compelled to go below the surface there is a good chance that we shall meet Him. Saul met Him in his single-minded obsession; Cleophas and the unknown disciple met Him in their sadness and bereavement. It would be impossible to relate all the various ways in which people have met the living Christ – 'indeed, I suppose that the world itself could not contain the books that would be written' (John 21:25). But the power of the New Testament events that have been recorded is to be found in the fact that they ring true today for countless other people who find themselves in the same shoes as Bartimaeus, Zacchaeus, Mary of Magdala, Peter, Cleopas, Paul and so on and so on, and so on . . .

So we do well to meditate carefully on the story of the road to Emmaus in St Luke's gospel, because in many ways it gives us the classic map references which are still clearly in evidence to this day. They were travelling. They were discussing. They were sad and they were in bereavement. It is just a fact that travelling (even today in fast aircraft) is a time when we are less cluttered and more open. Think of the eunuch in the book of the Acts of the Apostles (8:27ff); or Group Captain Cheshire on his way to drop the atomic bomb in Hiroshima. These are times when we collide with the living Christ.

Sometimes we do not recognize Him because He is in others. 'Saul, Saul, why are you persecuting *me*?' (Acts 9:4). For Saul it was Christ in those whom he was persecuting. For St Alban, the first English martyr, it was Christ in the face of a man whom he, Alban the soldier, was leading out to kill. For the Japanese prison officer it was Christ in the person of Bishop Wilson whom he had been torturing, and yet at the end of the war that same officer was confirmed as a Christian in Singapore Cathedral at the hands of that same bishop. For Augustine of Hippo it was Christ in the mind and intellect of little Ambrose, Bishop of Milan. For me it was Christ in the love and saintliness of an old parish priest, in the prayers of my mother, in the political concern shown during the Suez crisis by the Vicar of the University Church at Cambridge. For Cosmo Gordon Lang it was Christ in the peace of a holy place (Cuddesdon Parish Church), and in the saintly and quite remarkably beautiful face of Edward King, Bishop of Lincoln.

For Christ lives and reigns and still touches the hearts of men and women through and in others, in ways which most would find impossible to describe and in such a variety of ways that it is impossible to list or categorize them. Perhaps at the outset we do not recognize Him, or label Him. Only later, through reflection or through subsequent events, can we tell our story and say what happened to us on the road and 'how he was made known to *us*' (Luke 24:35). But essentially this encounter is personal: it is more than an idea or second-hand knowledge if it is really to be a turning point in our lives. It is acutely personal, never stereotyped; and seldom expected. Cleophas and the other disciple had heard rumours of resurrection, all the story of the women and what *they* had seen and told. Furthermore, an empty tomb was not enough in itself ('they were at the tomb early in the morning and did not find his body'). Neither a

Shroud of Turin – important and scientific though it is, and compelling though the arguments in its favour may be – nor any amount of archaeological discussion, will, in itself, bring living faith. Neither will second-hand reports – albeit of angels, who said that Jesus was alive. Hearing other people's opinions, even their testimonies – we know, at the end of the day ('for it was towards even'), that none of this will be evidence for faith. The only thing that turned those two disciples round and sent them back to Jerusalem was a personal encounter with the living, risen Christ. Then it was no longer a matter of hearsay – he say or she say – but rather they told what had happened to them on the road and how He was known to *them*.

But there are at least two other factors which help us in our contemporary encounters with Christ: the scriptures and the breaking of the bread. 'He interpreted to them in all the scriptures the things concerning himself' (Luke 24:27). The extraordinary thing about the Bible is that if you 'treat it like any other book, you will find that it is not like any other book' (Jowett). It is a living book, a charismatic book. Men and women throughout the ages have opened upon the words of this book and met the living Word in a personal encounter which has changed their lives. St Anthony of Egypt was in church and heard the words of the Gospel being read. Jesus said to him, 'If you would be perfect, go, sell what you possess and give to the poor, and you will have treasure in heaven; and come, follow me' (Matthew 19:21). He left all and followed literally the spirit of the Word which he had heard read as the gospel for the day.

St Augustine, in the year AD 386, on a warm summer afternoon in August, in a garden, heard the words: *tolle, lege,* supposedly on the lips of a little girl playing nearby. He picked up the Bible and read the words 'Let us conduct ourselves becomingly as in the day, not in revelling and drunkenness, not in debauchery and licentiousness, not in quarrelling and jealousy. But put on the Lord Jesus and make no provision for the flesh, to gratify its desires' (Romans 13:13f). Like a flash all his intellectual wrangling and moral ambivalence was behind him. The living Word of God changed his life. Similarly even in the book of the Acts of the Apostles we find the Ethiopian eunuch reading from the book of the prophet Isaiah, and it was the word in the book of the prophet which eventually was the vehicle whereby the Word was made known to him and enfleshed for him. This process has continued ever since. Archbishop Anthony Bloom tells of how he read the whole of St Mark's gospel at one sitting, and how formative that was in his own conversion. These and a million others would testify, along with Cleopas and that other disciple, in the words: 'Did not our hearts burn within us, while he talked with us on the road and while he opened to us the scriptures?' (verse 32). We shall meet and come to know the face of God in the Word of God, if we 'read' it, 'mark' it, 'learn' it and 'inwardly digest' it[1] in the spirit of God. It is not a magic book or an end in itself: rather it is a wonderful *means* of grace, pointing us again and again from the words to the Word with a living word of comfort, strength, challenge and confrontation if only we have 'ears to hear' and 'eyes to see' (Matthew 11:15).

It was, however, at table, as Jesus broke the bread that 'their eyes were opened and they recognized him' (verse 32). There can be no doubt from the New Testament record that 'the breaking of bread' was the characteristic activity of the early Church whenever it met for worship, as surely as it had become a characteristic of Jesus during His earthly ministry – so characteristic that they recognized Him at the very moment that He 'raised his eyes' to heaven (Matthew 11:15) and broke the bread. The Church has over the years found in this activity – the Holy Communion, the Eucharist, the Lord's Supper, the Breaking of Bread, the Liturgy, the Mass – a meeting point for the everyday Christian with the living Christ. Here, above all else, we are assured of His living presence, doing

the Lord's own thing on the Lord's day with the Lord's
people. It is very much in one sense the low-key, the
homely, unselfconscious way in which most Christians
most of the time have a personal encounter with their living
Lord. Of course the liturgy can become formalistic and
wrongly ritualistic and just (from our point of view) a
rather meaningless service.

Nevertheless, over the centuries it is this activity
supremely, for a thousand and one theological, practical
and even aesthetic reasons, which has become the place and
the way in which Christians have met and come to know
and to love the risen, living Christ. And this, not only in
great and moving eucharistic occasions, in vast and
beautiful cathedrals and churches, but also in a house
group, with two or three people, breaking bread together –
still, as on the road to Emmaus, men and women are
brought into the presence of the living Christ with their
eyes opened and recognize Him to be for them their
personal Lord and Saviour. The same could be said of the
other sacraments which the Church administers. God does
not need the sacraments but we do: outward and visible and
tangible signs of His love. Confirmation and first confession, a time of laying-on of hands and anointing –
thousands could testify that such moments were for them
times when, after years of church attendance, or without
church attendance at all, they could say that Christ had
made Himself known to them and they 'recognized' Him in
an unforgettable and formative way.

For it is at the end of the day, in definite places and with
two or three others, that the living risen Christ delights to
visit and 'abide with us' (verse 29). The corporate life of the
Church is important. Of course we are all individuals, but
as Christians our essential identity is our corporate life
within the Body of Christ. You cannot have Jesus without
the saints, but you must not try to have the saints without
Jesus. We know Christ best and experience Him in His
fullest presence in the fellowship of the saints and in His

Body, whose members we are invited to be. That does not mean that the Church has got the living Christ in its pocket, and of course there will be many who have a personal story to tell of a deeply moving and personal occasion when they were conscious of the presence of the risen Christ outside the environment of the Church. Because it is the Church on earth essentially bound up in its identity with the Body of Christ, that it is itself also perhaps one of the best vehicles through which people experience the presence of Christ.

Of course, it goes without saying that the Church on earth is not all that Christ intends it to be. There are many bad Christians. But nevertheless it is in the household of faith, in congregations and in the everyday life of the Church that I go on growing and travelling, and it is there that I most unselfconsciously and almost imperceptibly grow to 'know Him more clearly, love Him more dearly and follow Him more nearly, day by day'. There have been the special times, thank God: for some their first retreat, or their first confession; the gift of tongues or some particular moment of healing; there have been special places: a holy monastery, the church at Taizé or All Saints', Margaret Street, London where I personally rather specially came to love and to recognize Christ. But these are the hill tops and perforce most life has to be lived on the plains.

And that is why a *living* faith is whenever and wherever 'he appears to be going further' (verse 28). He will abide with us and for 'a little while' we see Him. But again 'a little while and we do not see' Him (John 16:16) because He is going to the Father and we must also travel and grow if we are to end up the right way round and in the right place. That is what the Ascension is all about. Nevertheless because of the Incarnation (and that is the complementary truth to the Ascension), renewal is localized in people and places. It is never evenly distributed. If you read the history of music in Vienna in the first thirty years of the

nineteenth century it is just not fair! There they *all* are:
Mozart, Beethoven, Schubert, Weber, Rossini, Paganini.
Western music was changed by a few people in those few
square miles outside Vienna woods. So it is with all
movements of renewal. There are undoubtedly holy places,
where He is known to abide. Renewal in the Church today
is localized and it is possible to think of it in guidebook and
even geographical terms. Of course He is everywhere, but
it is as though (for our sakes, not His) He is more in some
places than in others! Hence we should be pilgrims also in
the incarnate sense, not seeking to be above all that kind of
thing, and we should travel and go to the Holy Land and
Taizé and equally seek to meet people and faces such as
Mother Teresa of Calcutta, Archbishop Anthony Bloom
and Pope John Paul II. Shrines have their places and even
the record of lovers is not ashamed to draw attention to the
place where they met, the time of day and the very stones
which hallowed that meeting. There is no doubt whatever
that for St Francis the church at Damian was such a holy
place. And till their dying day the house in Emmaus would
be for Cleopas and the other disciple a very special place
indeed, like the upper room before and after that, and like
the temple in Jerusalem long before that. But – the truth of
the ascended Christ is that He always appears 'to be going
further'. Our encounters with the living Lord will be
moments we cherish – and they will locate for us places
which we cherish for the rest of our lives. Yet we must
move on and travel again, for here we have no abiding city,
but rather as strangers and pilgrims we are seeking the city
of God, where with all God's saints, old and new alike we
shall see Him. We shall see 'the river of the water of life,
bright as crystal, flowing from the throne of God and of the
Lamb through the middle of the street of the city', but
there will be 'no temple in the city, for its temple is the
Lord God the Almighty and the Lamb', yet there we shall
'see his face and his name shall be on' *our* foreheads. And
the night shall be no more 'for *we* shall need no longer' lamp

or sun, for the Lord will be *our* 'light' and 'we' shall reign
for ever (Revelation 22).

So through the journey on earth the ruthless repetitive
command of the Church is always the same: 'Go forth upon
thy journey Christian soul.'

NOTES

Introduction

1 G. K. Chesterton, *Orthodoxy*, Bodley Head, 1942, p. 48.
2 J. E. Bode, verse 5 of Hymn 'O Jesus, I have promised', *English Hymnal* 577.
3 Martin Thornton, *English Spirituality*, S.P.C.K., London, 1963, p. 3.
4 Prayer Book Collect for Second Sunday in Advent.

PART ONE

Chapter One

1 J. H. Newman, *An Essay on the Development of Christian Doctrine*, Penguin Books, 1974, p. 100.
2 H. F. Lyte, verse 2 of Hymn 'Abide with me', *English Hymnal* 363.

Chapter Two

1 Shakespeare, *Macbeth*, Act V, Scene 5.
2 Ian Currie, *You Cannot Die*, Hamlyn, 1978, and Raymond A. Moody, *Life after Life*, Bantam Books, USA, 1975.
3 William Temple, *Readings in St John's Gospel* (First and Second Series), Macmillan, London, 1955, p. 37.
4 Christopher Booker, *The Neophiliacs. A Study of the Revolution in English Life in the Fifties and Sixties*, Fontana, 1970.
5 Thomas Arnold, *Principles of Church Reform*, first published in 1832.
6 William Temple, *Readings in St John's Gospel*, pp. 226f.

7 G. K. Chesterton, *Orthodoxy*, Bodley Head, 1942.
8 C. S. Lewis, *The Allegory of Love*, Oxford University Press, 1938.
9 Prayer Book Collect for Fourth Sunday after Trinity.

Chapter Three

1 Lennon and McCartney, 'Nowhere Man'.
2 Søren Kierkegaard, *Purity of Heart is to Will One Thing*, first written in 1846, Fontana, 1961.
3 Thomas Merton, *No Man is an Island*, Hollis and Carter, London, 1955, p. xvi; Burns and Oates, London

Chapter Four

1 Sir J. Bowring, opening verse of 'In the Cross of Christ I glory', *English Hymnal* 409.
2 Augustine saw the basic symbolism of baptism as fundamental to all his subsequent life and preaching as a Christian and a bishop. 'And so you put on not us but Christ. I did not ask you whether you turned towards me, but towards the living God: not whether you believed in me, but in the Father and the Son and the Holy Spirit' (*outra litt. Pet.*, 3, 8, 9).
'The symbolism by which in his renunciation a man relinquishes night and the setting sun, and turns towards the light' *(Enarratio* in Psalm 76:4).
3 Laurens van der Post, *Patterns of Renewal*, published by Pendle Hall, 1962, p. 9.
4 1 Samuel 10:26, and used as text for enthronement sermon by Archbishop Michael Ramsey in 1961.
5 Oscar Wilde, *The Ballad of Reading Gaol*

> Ah! happy they whose hearts can break and peace and pardon win!
> How else may man make straight his plan and cleanse his soul from sin?
> How else but through a broken heart may Lord Christ enter in?

6   Margery Williams, *The Velveteen Rabbit*, published by
    Heinemann in 1970 but written some 50 years earlier.

Chapter Five

1   Michael Howard and Peter Ford, *The True History of
    the Elephant Man*, Allison and Busby Ltd, London,
    1980.
    Bernard Pomerance, *The Elephant Man* (play), 1979.
2   Prayer Book Collect for Fourth Sunday after Trinity.
3   C. S. Lewis, *The Great Divorce*, Fount Paperbacks,
    1972, pp. 27f.
4   St Augustine, *City of God*, edited by David Knowles,
    Pelican Classics, 1972, p. 1091.
5   'In our day of thanksgiving', verse 4, *Hymns Ancient
    and Modern*.

PART TWO

Chapter One

1   T. S. Eliot, 'Burnt Norton' III: *The Four Quartets*.
2   It is repeated like an antiphon or chorus: viz. Genesis 1
    verses 10, 12, 18, 21, 25.
3   Don Marquis, *Archy and Mehitabel: the Lesson of the
    Moth*.
4   C. S. Lewis, 'Transposition and other addresses' in *The
    Weight of Glory*, Geoffrey Bles, London, 1949, p. 21.
5   Gilbert and Sullivan, *Trial By Jury*.
6   George Herbert, 'Teach me, my God and King', verse
    2, *English Hymnal* 484.
7   Shakespeare, *King Lear*.

Chapter Two

1   Eric Berne, *The Games People Play*, Penguin, 1964.
2   Simon Tugwell, OP, *Did You Receive the Spirit?*,
    Darton, Longman and Todd, London, 1972, pp. 97f.
3   Prayer of John Ward, MP for Dagenham many years

ago, and quoted in W. E. Sangster, *Teach Me to Pray*, Epworth Press, London, 1951, p. 13.

4 George Herbert, 'Love' from *The Temple* poems.

5 George Herbert, 'King of Glory, King of Peace', verse 3, *English Hymnal* 424.

6 John Donne, Holy Sonnets xiv, *Poems*, J. M. Dent & Sons Ltd, London, 1931, p. 254.

7 Julian of Norwich.

8 Emily E. S. Elliott, 'Thou didst leave thy throne and thy kingly crown', Refrain, *English Hymnal* 585.

Chapter Three

1 C. S. Lewis, 'The Weight of Glory' in *Transposition and Other Addresses*, p. 24.

2 Teilhard de Chardin, *Le Milieu Divin*, Fontana/Fount, London, 1964, p. 92.

3 St Augustine, *Confessions*, Book 1, Chapter 1.

4 'My Song is Love Unknown', *With One Voice*, 257, Collins, 1979.

5 T. S. Eliot, 'East Coker' III.

6 W. Cowper, 'O for a closer walk with God', verse 3, *English Hymnal* 445.

7 St John of the Cross.

8 C. S. Lewis, 'The Weight of Glory' in *Transposition and Other Addresses*, p. 21.

9 J. Clarke, 'Immortal love for ever full,' verse 7, *English Hymnal* 408.

Chapter Four

1 Prayer of Oblation, Book of Common Prayer.

2 For a discussion of the difference between 'nearness *by distance*' and 'nearness *by approach*' see C. S. Lewis, *The Four Loves*, Fontana/Fount, London, 1963, pp. 13f.

3 Oscar Wilde, *The Ballad of Reading Gaol*.

4 Luke 23:34. They are in fact parallel imperfect tenses: 'As they were crucifying him, he kept on saying.'

H. Collins, 'Jesu, my Lord, my God, my all', *English Hymnal* 417.

Chapter Five

I. Watts, 'When I survey the wondrous cross', verse 5, *English Hymnal* 107.

'In our day of thanksgiving', v. 3.

Equus, by Peter Shaffer, W. H. Draper.

'The duteous day now closeth' by P. Gerhardt, *English Hymnal* 278.

George Herbert, 'King of glory, King of peace,' verse 2, *English Hymnal* 424.

Chapter Six

T. S. Eliot, 'East Coker' V, last line from *Four Quartets*.

'Rise up, O men of God', by William Pierson Merrill, *Methodist Hymn Book* 585, v. 3.

Sir J. Bowring, 'In the Cross of Christ I glory,' *English Hymnal* 409.

EPILOGUE

Prayer Book Collect for Second Sunday in Advent.

Also available in Fount Paperbacks

Journey for a Soul
GEORGE APPLETON

'Wherever you turn in this inexpensive but extraordinarily valuable paperback you will benefit from sharing this man's pilgrimage of the soul.'

Methodist Recorder

The Imitation of Christ
THOMAS A KEMPIS

After the Bible, this is perhaps the most widely read book in the world. It describes the way of the follower of Christ – an intensely practical book, which faces the temptations and difficulties of daily life, but also describes the joys and helps which are found on the way.

Autobiography of a Saint:
Thérèse of Lisieux
RONALD KNOX

'Ronald Knox has bequeathed us a wholly lucid, natural and enchanting version . . . the actual process of translating seems to have vanished, and a miracle wrought, as though St Teresa were speaking to us in English . . . his triumphant gift to posterity.'

G. B. Stern, The Sunday Times

Wrestling with Christ
LUIGI SANTUCCI

'This is a most unusual book, a prolonged meditation of the life of Christ using many changing literary forms, dialogue, description, addresses to Christ, passages of self-communing. It is written by a Christian passionately concerned that everyone should know Jesus Christ.'

Catholic Herald

Also available in Fount Paperbacks

The Foundations of New Testament Christology
R. H. FULLER

'A most important book . . . with a splendidly imaginative grasp of the way in which the Gospel unfolded as it was planted in different soils . . . this book will remain a major contribution to Christological origins.'

New Christian

Jesus – The Man Who Lives
MALCOLM MUGGERIDGE

'The book is excellently produced and beautifully illustrated . . . it bears witness to Malcolm Muggeridge's deep convictions, his devotion to the person of Jesus.'

Mervyn Stockwood
Church of England Newspaper

Jesus Rediscovered
MALCOLM MUGGERIDGE

'. . . one of the most beautifully written, perverse, infuriating, enjoyable and moving books of the year.'

David Edwards, Church Times

Jesus the Jew
GEZA VERMES

'A painstakingly researched, meticulously documented, cogently reasoned and eminently readable new book . . . it represents an important step forward in New Testament study which henceforth scholars, even if they do not wholly agree with it, will not be able to ignore.'

Times Literary Supplement

Fount Paperbacks

Fount is one of the leading paperback publishers of religious books and below are some of its recent titles.

- ☐ SQUARE WORDS IN A ROUND WORLD Eric Kemp 95p
- ☐ THE HOLY SPIRIT Billy Graham 95p
- ☐ REACHING OUT Henri Nouwen 95p
- ☐ DEATH & AFTER: WHAT WILL REALLY HAPPEN?
    H. J. Richards £1.25
- ☐ GO AN EXTRA MILE Michael Wood 95p
- ☐ HAPPY FAMILIES Anthony Bullen 95p
- ☐ THE NEW INQUISITION? SCHILLEBEECKX AND KÜNG
    Peter Hebblethwaite £1.25
- ☐ CHRISTIANITY AND OTHER RELIGIONS
    John Hick & Brian Hebblethwaite £1.50
- ☐ TOWARDS THE DAWN Clifford Hill £1.25
- ☐ THE POPE FROM POLAND John Whale £1.50
- ☐ THE FAITH OF AN ANGLICAN Gilbert Wilson £2.95
- ☐ PRAYER FOR PILGRIMS Sheila Cassidy £1.50

All Fount paperbacks are available at your bookshop or news-agent, or they can also be ordered by post from Fount Paperbacks, Cash Sales Department, G.P.O. Box 29, Douglas, Isle of Man, British Isles. Please send purchase price, plus 10p per book. Customers outside the U.K. send purchase price, plus 12p per book. Cheque, postal or money order. No currency.

NAME (Block letters) _____

ADDRESS _____

_____

_____